Sports fitness for women

Sports fitness for women

Elizabeth and Ken Day

B.T. Batsford Ltd   London

Thanks to **Ann Hazel** marathon runner and P.E. teacher; **Claire Tancock**, gymnast and sprinter, and **Ann Quinlan**, games player and all-round athlete.

Photographs by Menor of Sawbridgeworth

© Elizabeth and Ken Day 1986
First published 1986

ISBN 0 7134 4692 7

Typeset by Tek-Art Ltd, Kent
and printed in Great Britain by
Anchor Brendon Ltd
Tiptree, Essex
for the publishers
B.T. Batsford Ltd.
4 Fitzhardinge Street
London W1H 0AH

Contents

Introduction

Women in sport are now a serious force in world competition, and the domination by men of world-class sport is threatened. At a professional level, the quality and quantity of high money earning women is quite remarkable, and the publicity attracted has led to a media glamorisation of health, fitness and vitality.

In order to have excellence at the top of the world sporting scene there must be a huge base of regular players at a lesser level; these regular participants provide the next generation of stars.

There is no doubt that the number of people taking part in sport at all levels has vastly increased: paying spectators have now become paying participants. Indeed, sport in its loosest terms has become a national preoccupation. Good facilities have been made available for all to enjoy, and the private clubs are far out-numbered by sports and leisure centres which offer multitudes of sports under one roof.

The Central Council for Physical Recreation (C.C.P.R.) has a nationwide policy of 'Sport for All', and the public are encouraged to 'have a go'. Invariably sports centres offer a family package which invites us to enjoy our leisure time in a sporting atmosphere. Mass media implores us to 'work-out' or 'fight the flab', but opinions vary greatly as to the best way to get fit. Many commercial concerns offer the panacea for a few pence or pounds, but there is only one true method: to increase general condition it is necessary to embark upon a scheme of regular and progressive exercise. All other techniques are purely supplementary.

Since each person is unique in every way, no one method will work for everyone, and a certain amount of experiment is necessary to discover what is right for you. The schedules and guidance provided should be studied and tried in order to get the right balance of exercise.

The present national interest in fitness and health is not aimed chiefly at sports fitness: it is more a medical warning shot at people who may be prone to heart problems and other difficulties caused by lack of regular exercise.

Over recent years there has been a large increase in leisure time for many people, and out-of-the-home leisure activities are becoming a more serious part of our everyday lives. Women are involving themselves in sports for health, enjoyment and physical improvement, and indeed the enjoyment from taking part is superseding that from watching.

The fun gained from sport cannot be fully explained. It is slightly different for each individual. We all laugh at various things, but may have tastes which vary greatly. Like humour, sport has some core elements. Perhaps the greatest of these is the sheer exhilaration of feeling fit and healthy. The sensation of health and stamina above the general level is a very deep and pleasurable knowledge. No matter how old or in what physical shape you are, there is always the personal satisfaction of being fit. Exercise also promotes a more immediate, and attractive side-effect which can best be described as a 'high'. A hormone release is provoked during vigorous work-out which brings on a feeling of elation and happiness.

Top calibre gymnasts and swimmers are reported as being 'over the hill' by their late twenties, which makes you wonder what they will do in a sporting sense for the next 50 years. Sport and advancing age is rather misunderstood. The body maturity sequence has been investigated, and in all but a few cases nature has arranged for the bones and tissues to be at their best, not just in youth, but for the most of a person's truly active life. In other words, there is no reason to offer age as a reason (or an excuse) for not getting fit. Natural stamina improves into the middle years of life.

There are numerous sports clubs which reach a reasonable standard of performance; sports fitness training is designed to raise these levels. Team games depend upon a unique blend of skills and abilities. Too many clubs produce a fixtures list and not a programme of fitness training. Happily the days of playing sport to get fit are almost over. The maxim nowadays is – get fit to play games.

This book is intended to guide you in the direction of fitness for sport in general. The methods recommended are tried and tested, but they will work only if you do. This is an opportunity to plan a programme with progressive schedules and imaginative exercises.

If for any reason illness, injury, or other problems are a worry, it is advisable to consult your doctor before embarking upon a serious fitness programme. Many people are deterred by the whole idea of improving fitness because of a past history of medical problems. General fitness sessions will, with care and planning, form a basis for general health improvement. The functions of the body respond to work. The circulation of blood created by strengthening the heart beat, and the improvement of breathing are the two most valuable health and fitness building blocks. As soon as breathlessness due to exercise is reduced, you can safely say that you are getting fit.

ATTITUDES TO WOMEN IN SPORT

Women who take sport seriously, not necessarily to an international, or even national, level, may well find that planning the family timetable is as important as planning their training sessions. Keep-fit classes are an acceptable pastime for mothers, although they will often have to hire a baby-sitter, since their husbands are 'unable' to hold the fort for those few hours; but how many men would find it acceptable to have a wife who spent every Saturday afternoon or Sunday morning out on a sports field?

Whilst women are unlikely to compete against men in the majority of sports, this is no reason to disregard the importance of fitness for women. Even in a household where both partners are actively involved in sport, there is usually an unwritten agreement that the husband's training is more important than his wife's. This attitude will only be changed by *women* — who must assert their needs and ensure that they have a reasonable amount of time and opportunity to fulfil their fitness or sports programme.

SPORTS CLOTHES

Fashion and sport are inextricably bound together, and the inevitable dangers lie in looking for garments which are chic but not really practical. The right clothing for sport ought to be thought of as working garb. This may give the impression of dour, drab, over-suits and baggy cotton shorts and shirts, but nothing is further from reality: colours and styles are virtually infinite. It is important to know how to choose clothing which will be very practical and also an absolute pleasure to wear.

Fabrics should be stretchy and absorbent, which means that denim is useless for sport. When dressing for training it is best to build up layers so that you can strip off gradually during the warm-up, and replace clothing whilst warming down. The weight and type of kit will depend on the weather and the season, and a decent all-weather suit will be useful for wet weather training. Avoid the cheap nylon suits which can cause severe sweating and are often not really waterproof.

The wrong clothing and footwear are the root causes of sweat rash, jogger's nipple (and stretch marks), athlete's foot, vaginal thrush and, ultimately, the end of your sport.

A well-structured sports bra adjusted to reduce bounce is essential. Never train without a bra. All underclothes must be absorbent and afford reasonable cover so that there is no chafing. Minute underwear may seem glamorous but it is very impractical. Cotton socks are recommended for all sports: they are invariably quite soft and will absorb sweat.

It is easy to look the part without being a slave to fashion. Most of the fashionable clothing is perfectly practical for sport, although, as far as colour schemes go, do consider your measurements before wearing pastel colours, as they are the most unflattering choice for the fuller figure.

Always wear clean clothes, especially against the skin, for freshness and health. If you look good and feel fashionable you can perform your sports without worrying about critics in the audience.

1 Exercise in general

What is being fit?

Let it be said right from the start that no matter how fit you are, there is always room for improvement. In general, people are in a low state of physical fitness, but there is, however, a strong desire to be fit and healthy.

In order to say how fit a person is at any time we must be able to compare their present level with data from the past. Measurements of fitness are not easy to record unless you are under expert guidance. Everybody knows the sensation of feeling healthy, in good condition – fit. It is also true to say that the moment an unfit or unhealthy period looms up, our senses and responses quickly recognise it. What is there to notice in the way of signs of fitness? You are seldom breathless – even under stress. Muscles do not ache after lifting and carrying. The skin and hair feel clean and fresh. General health and vitality is high. In short, you are fit and happy.

The next question is: fit for what? Most sports require very specific training to reach a high level; in this situation highly developed techniques of training are used. The general need in most sporting lives is to be fit enough to enjoy and at times excel in our chosen sports. A small amount of training above that which is normal has a remarkable effect upon our abilities. When basic fitness is raised, special skills become easier to learn and repeat.

The elements of physical fitness are stamina, strength, speed, flexibility and skill. Each one complements the other. It is better to balance them out in proportions to suit your sport, and interests.

Stamina fitness is when the heart and lungs are capable of working hard for long periods. A distance runner and a swimmer have high levels of this quality.

Strength is one of those characteristics which nature gives in larger quantities to some than to others. Muscles strengthen when they are worked, and anyone can increase muscular strength. The amount of muscle and its quality are the major limiting factors. Large, muscular, heavily built people tend to be strong, and can lift heavy weights. Smaller frames with lighter muscles do not have the same sort of strength. In general, women are not built strongly because nature has not devised them as a work horse. Feminine muscles are strong, however, and become stronger without being bulky.

Anyone who can move quickly is automatically a strong individual. Speed is an essential element of most sports. If you are able to control speed, then it is of greatest use. Practice of any sport increases the ability to use speed without great tense effort, and therefore the quality of movement and the muscular effort involved are balanced.

Some people, particularly gymnasts, seem almost to be made of rubber: they have extremely flexible joints and pliant muscles. Most of us, however, lose our childlike flexibility in our mid teens, from which time the joints of our bodies work in only the convenient middle range. Exercises to increase range of movement are essential to improvement in sports. After all, good flexibility aids breathing and circulation. It also prevents common injuries, permits easy use of the muscles and allows skills to be quickly learnt.

Skill is an element in general sports fitness which is too often ignored. It is taken for granted that an expert in gymnastics or tennis has a high level of skill as well as a very deep basic level of fitness. The need to improve fitness and skill go hand in hand. If a skill is repeated many times, fatigue sets in and the quality of movements begins to deteriorate. However, in order to enjoy a sport fully you must be fit, and reasonably skilful, since when the fitness fails, so does the skill. The answer to this apparent dilemma is that skill training ought to be practised when you are fresh. Basic fitness work is best performed after the skill session has been performed.

This brings us to the question of how to do exercises for basic fitness. The mindless pumping of arms and legs to reduce yourself to a redfaced, puffing wreck is pointless. Training is designed to create special results, and it is very important, therefore, that all the exercises are performed with quality, rather than inaccurate quantity. Beginners may doubt the need for care and perfection during the initial getting fit period, but be advised that quality of movement has a far more effective role to play than many incorrect repetitions.

It should not be forgotten that the beginner will have some difficulty in managing some movements, but the advice of the old axiom cannot be bettered: practice makes perfect. These two words are the keystones of how to do exercises. After a set of really accurate movements there is the satisfaction of knowing that the job is well done, and the results will be quicker and longer lasting. Sloppily performed movements can cause niggling injuries and frustration. The whole point of taking exercise is to improve general condition and health. Treat the schedules with the same reverence as you would medicines. The pride of achievement at the end of a good session is a measure of your efforts.

Good muscle tone is the control of figure, posture and shape of the body. Sagging muscles create a floppy figure, whilst muscles that are under control give the beauty and poise demonstrated by dancers, gymnasts, models and all sports people. The joy of having a good shape, whatever your size, is directly connected with muscle tone. In this case the muscles do not have to be bulky: quite the opposite gives the best results, and fit muscles have good natural tension.

Tummy muscles which are taut and flat are healthy. It is possible to have excellent muscular condition whilst still carrying a certain amount of fat; in fact, for women it is perfectly natural to carry a fat pad on the tummy. There can be unfounded worries created by this layer of tissue. If the muscle tone is good and the tummy muscles are capable of 25-30 fast sit-ups, the fat deposit should cause no concern. Good tummy muscles will improve digestion, and therefore aid general fitness.

POSTURE

Posture is a social grace as well as being an integral part of fitness. The structure of the human body is best held erect with straight shoulders, flat stomach and the bottom tucked in. The immediate gain from this shape is easier movement, better breathing and circulation, and, of course, a greater pride in your physique; thus muscles are essential to good poise, posture and shape. Sagging and poorly maintained muscles are one of the obvious signs of an unfit person, and may result in round shoulders (kyphosis), a bowed back (lordosis), a droopy bustline and protruding bottom.

General fitness training will not make the body out of proportion: quite the opposite. The female physique has exactly the same muscles as a man, but they are not as bulky or as powerful, and therefore any 'male' exercise is also good for women provided the movement is slightly adapted to suit the female frame.

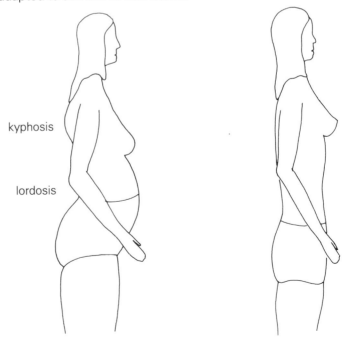

kyphosis

lordosis

1 Bad posture (the slump) and good posture (the tuck)

Muscles require a stimulus to improve their tension and shape. Fitness training is the spark which sets alight the response in tissues. The blood flow to the muscles is increased during exercise, and the supply of nutrients and oxygen to the fibres allows the muscles to work hard. Scientists are still trying to discover exactly what causes muscle growth, but happily it does occur. Even more beneficial is the fact that muscle tissues do not have to grow to enormous size in order to be fit and strong.

People with good and attractive physiques have well shaped and evenly balanced muscles. Some sports tend to encourage different parts of the body to develop quickly, but it takes an extremely intense type of training to create this sort of development. Women can build muscles but seldom to the level seen in men's physiques. There may be a fear of becoming grotesquely built, but only in the most unusual circumstances and with prolonged effort will the female body develop the same type of muscle definition associated with male body-builders. There should be no fear of becoming 'muscle bound' and grotesque from doing any of the exercises in this book; and whilst the sleek flat tummy and neatly defined physique cannot be achieved without work, this book has no exercises which will build mighty bulk and bulging biceps.

MUSCLE TENSIONING

A remarkable effect can be achieved by holding muscles under tension. Muscles are working when they shorten and harden, which usually means that joints and limbs are moving. It is possible to tense muscles without actually doing exercises in the traditional sense. An example of this is to press the hands together in front of the chest. The muscles of the chest and shoulders contract and harden. They are therefore being tensed and are trying to shorten. If this tension is held for about eight seconds at a reasonable pressure, the blood supply to the tissues is increased, and, as a result, the muscles improve in strength and general condition.

This has been recognised in body culture and, over the years, has been commercially exploited. Various machines have been developed which are supposed to aid muscle tensing exercises, but it is quite unnecessary to use any sophisticated gadgets to enjoy the profits of held muscle tension. The two exercises illustrated in Fig. 2 are the easiest ones to practise. The benefits are quite quickly noticeable. The chest and shoulder muscles respond very easily to treatment. It is, after all, the pectoral muscles under the breast tissues that give the shape and poise to a good bustline.

The press or pull effort on the muscles must be at about two-thirds maximum pressure and this is held for a steady count to eight. Muscles in the chest and shoulders will respond by hardening and thus are working. As a result of this work the tissues will improve in general condition.

In hospitals, physiotherapists and doctors use this technique to aid recovery. Patients are taught to clench or tense their muscles to improve circulation and muscle condition. All the muscles can be worked with this technique. It is only a supplement to other training methods.

Anyone in a sedentary job would do well to improvise regular muscle tensioning exercises. If your work means sitting at a desk, there is a tendency to lose good muscle condition and suffer with a stiffening of the joints often resulting in back or shoulder ache. The circulatory system has very little to do whilst telephoning or typing, and so at regular periods during the day various muscle groups can be unobtrusively tensed. When you are skilled at this technique you can hold muscle tension without anyone knowing what you are doing.

2 Pull, push muscle tension

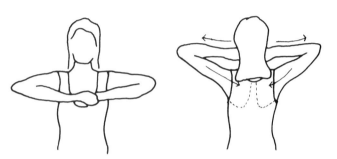

There is one particular word which has taken the fitness headlines by storm: aerobics. The effect of aerobics has always been a major part of any fitness programme; it is the word alone that has not been in common use until recently. The meaning is simple: any activity which causes enormous use of oxygen in the body. The heart will beat faster, and is kept at a reasonably high rate. At the same time, the breathing has to work hard to keep pace as far as possible with the need for oxygen, and thus the basic heart and lungs (cardiovascular) system is in use. The internal system of circulation and breathing is put through its paces. It is a basic fitness system. Care must be used to grade the difficulty and severity of the first few aerobic sessions. Running in all its forms is perhaps the best type of aerobic exercise.

The opposite of aerobic work is an-aerobic. In this case there is no oxygen supply-and-demand problem. The muscles are used without causing a puffing, heavy breathing, panting response. Exercises of this type are muscle building, and toning. Sequences of movements to increase flexibility are also in this category.

By combining these elements in balanced proportions the best results will be achieved.

SOMATOTYPES

Each of us has a slightly different type of physique. Most people who are good at sport seem to have bodies which are quite muscular and carry a comparatively small amount of fat.

There is scientific study of physiques called somatotyping. Physiques can be studied, measured and categorised. The amount of fat, muscle, bone, sinew, etc., is calculated and, as a result of this, a named category is assigned to the individual (*Fig. 3*): rounded physiques are called *endomorphs*; muscular square bodies are called *mesomorphs*, and linear-shaped bodies are called *ectomorphs*.

3 Somatotypes

mesomorph   ectomorph   endomorph

It is not possible to assign a somatotype accurately to anyone without extensive measurement and study, but people who are sport inclined tend to be mesomorphs. This does not mean that they are all muscle and bone without a balanced quantity of the other elements: in fact, everyone has a blend of the three extremes.

Long distance runners will tend to be ectomorphs with a good muscle content; swimmers tend to be mesomorphic, as are gymnasts, (although it is difficult to imagine heavily-built swimmers gracefully performing back flips). The body type has similar blends of the basic elements to the gymnast, and it is only the form of training which gives a different visual effect.

Extreme endomorphs, or fat people, are not suited to sport. A progressive training sequence will change the shape but not the somatotype.

It is, therefore, safe to say that in all but a very few cases, fitness training will cause the body to respond. This response is normally a reduction in fat and a slight increase of muscle, and the obvious improvement in general health. The unique nature of our bodies also means that the rate of improvement will be individual, so that any comparisons between training partners will have to take into account any difference in somatotype.

WARMING-UP – WARMING-DOWN

All training schedules and sports should be preceded by a period of warming-up. This is a safety measure more than anything else: it is a necessity to prevent pulled muscles and associated injuries. Warming-up prepares the body and senses for the work ahead. On very hot days, or when working in a warm gymnasium, the amount of time spent getting ready will be shorter than on a cold day. The best idea is to have a routine which follows a sequence.

The blood must flow, the lungs must open up and take in oxygen. The muscles and joints must test themselves out, quite gently at first.

How can this best be accomplished? To get the heart and lungs going there is nothing better than a run. It is not necessary to go far or fast. Running increases the heart beat and gets the breathing going. If the run causes distress then some adjustment is needed to find the right amount.

The next part of the routine is to prepare the body muscles and joints for action. (The formula must be to use progressively more demanding stretches and exercises.) Always start with general movements and then change to specific exercises.

A good warm-up, therefore, could follow a pattern of this type:

1 Jogging for 5 minutes
2 Bending and stretching, i.e. forward bend followed by high upward stretches
3 Arm swinging in all directions
4 Leg swings
5 Lunges and hurdle sitting
6 Side bends
7 Hip circling
8 Trunk curling from side to side
9 On the spot fast run for 45 seconds

This will take between 15 and 20 minutes, and you are now ready to begin your training session.

At the end of a fitness training session you must warm-down. The body will have been under some pressure. Indeed, you will have been driving and striving for a high level of effort. If a sudden halt is used as a finish to a session there will be stiff muscles and the chance of suffering simple injury from cramp. Warming-down gently slows the invigorated body and sluices out the waste products (lactic acid) from the muscles. It also allows the heart rate to reduce its pace. It is often best to put on extra clothing at the end of a session so that body temperature is lost slowly.

Below is a warming-down sequence, although the content may depend upon the severity of the work-out session.

1 A gentle 5 minutes jog
2 Hamstring stretching

3   Two minutes jog

4   Easy body circles

5   One minute jog

6   Gentle arm circles

Don't forget to finish off with a warm bath or shower – this not only eliminates the sweat you will have built up, but also acts as a final muscle relaxant.

Invariably the exercises for warming up can be used gently to warmdown. Some of the exercises are also of value as a regular part of the training session. The preparation of body and mind for a tough session is very important to get the best out of yourself.

Complete recovery from a good work-out may take several hours, and a comparitive beginner could feel the effects for a day or two. However, after regular sessions over a period of some weeks, the response of the body becomes conditioned to dealing with any after-effects.

SENSIBLE EATING

A great deal has been published over the years about what you should and should not eat, and to many people the word 'diet' only means cutting down on food. Sports fitness can be impaired by poor eating habits, and a good balanced diet with sensible eating patterns should go hand in hand with general health and fitness. A great degree of self-control may need to be exercised – choosing salad instead of fish and chips, and avoiding too many stodgy snacks – but the rewards will be self-evident and worthwhile. You should eat plenty of fresh fruit and vegetables, make sure you drink plenty of fluid and watch your alcohol intake. It is so simple to get it right, and equally easy to stray from the sensible course. If the quantity and the quality are balanced, then no special forms of diet or foods are needed. Vigorous training causes hunger and this alone can create a dilemma, but it is absolutely unnecessary to increase food intake if a good and varied diet is followed. Regular training helps the body to use food very efficiently, whilst also reducing the fat built up from over-eating. Fit people are seldom weighty, although muscle is heavier than fat. A slim-built fit body may be surprisingly heavy because the proportion of muscle tissue to that of fat will increase slightly. The unwanted and useless fat deposits are burnt up by regular work.

The word 'fat' has many unpleasant associations, and is rarely used in a non-critical context. Some fat deposits on the body are natural, however, and therefore quite normal, while excessively large fatty deposits are a nuisance in many ways. In the course of getting fit, the general body shape will alter. Probably the most dramatic change is the rapid trimming away of a great deal of unwanted fat. Healthy active bodies have a shape and form which is attractive to the eye and a joy for the person who is fit.

The majority of people in the Western world eat too much fat, cholestrol and sugar and not enough fibre, although ever-increasing awareness of this fact is having positive results. Meat is a tasty and satisfying food, but full of fats, and therefore a reduction in the amount of red meat consumed is very highly recommended. It is also a good idea to eat only lean cuts or to remove the fat before cooking. Poultry and fish, plus the great variety of pulses now available, are all healthier alternatives.

It is not easy to change eating habits, particularly in a family situation, and it may be necessary to wean yourself from the habits of a lifetime.

Vegetables offer most of the proteins and complex nutritional substances needed for healthy living. An added bonus from eating greens is the cleansing of the lower intestine. The cooking of vegetables must not be overdone: greatest value is retained by quick cooking, preferably steaming, rather than long-term boiling or soaking.

A fitness programme will be much more effective if your diet and general eating habits are planned and designed with health in mind.

A BALANCED FITNESS

The sporting world is becoming very specialised, and science and physiology have been combined to produce the optimum performance from top athletes. In these cases there is not a balanced fitness, but more a high peak in one particular aspect.

The best situation, unless special circumstances exist, is to have a balanced fitness, i.e. where the elements of stamina, speed, strength, flexibility and skill are in proportion. This may well mean that after careful assessment of either your needs, or weaknesses, you are led to work at particular aspects rather than all methods. For example, if stamina is a problem, then the chosen schedule will differ from one for someone seeking speed or flexibility.

The balance has to be regularly checked. A routine may well have a certain emphasis, and once the level of fitness has been improved, or raised, it may be necessary to change the schedules to deal with the next problem. At this point be warned. It is easy to follow sessions that you enjoy, but it is possible that they might not be hard enough for optimum benefit, or even too hard, risking injury. Constant assessment and modification are the answer, and you will find that planning and patience are needed, as well as effort.

Anyone who is overweight should avoid muscle strengthening exercises in favour of basic fitness sessions, and aerobic work. In this way the balance will be achieved.

Planning your fitness programme involves taking into account a number of external factors: certain times of the year will be more or less conducive to outdoor activities, and, since most sports are seasonal, the annual peaks and troughs must be considered. Since it is impossible to retain peak fitness throughout the year, careful planning is needed to ensure that optimum performance is not wasted out of season.

With this in mind, an annual plan can be based upon each sport, allowing for a build-up period to the beginning of the season. There should be an initial phase of steady work before full-out effort is tried. A peak of fitness cannot be maintained for more than a fortnight, after which there is a tendency to go 'off the boil'. Several peaks of fitness can be reached each year. Most sports have a tournament or high season during the course of the year, and an inventive club or individual will recognise this and plan to be at peak fitness at the right time.

A method to get these results is to plan the sporting calendar and allow a minimum of ten weeks to gain basic fitness. This is then followed by three weeks of hard specialised work for extra sharpening. The peak should last for about two weeks with a normal training load. Heavy, hard, sessions should be avoided at a peak.

At regular intervals there should be a softening of the sessions to allow a certain amount of recovery. No one can train at full effort continuously, and the peaks and troughs of fitness can be structured to suit your sport. A balance of periods of hard and soft training can soon be established, and these cycles of training, as they are called, are in regular use with athletes in particular. In this sport the season is becoming less well defined, and a close study of the calendar makes it necessary to plan at least one year in advance.

Achieving a balanced fitness, therefore, involves more than just taking exercise. Individual human differences and the variety of sports require sophisticated and planned methods of fitness improvement. There is also no fixed time-scale for getting fit, and no real means of testing what is achieved.

A person who normally has a very active life will appear to be fit. In this case a quite vigorous system of schedules can be used immediately. The initial results will show a rapid improvement: in all cases the first level of success is quick and relatively easy to attain. The muscles and tissues of the body react very swiftly to a regular work-out at first. When the natural processes in the body have adjusted to taking regular exercise, the rate of improvement tends to slow down. Even an increase of intensity is no guarantee of a similar raising of the level of fitness when compared to the first spurt.

It is true, therefore, that very unfit people will appear to enjoy a fast initial improvement. Beyond this point there is the automatic levelling in the rate of progress.

A drop out from fitness training can be the temptation when you reach the sticking point. There appears to be no incentive to go on. Now is the time to be inventive and begin to build schedules which are fun and effective. By this time most people will be regular, habitual, participants. There can be a feeling of guilt if you have not done your session regularly.

In brief, your commitment to getting fit will be tested. A decision is necessary as to how much time can be set aside for training and taking part in sport. There is evidence to suggest that regular fitness fans become quite depressed if they do not work-out each day. Indeed, many treat the sessions as the high point in their personal lives. They relish the whole build-up, taking part and cooling down.

The time-scale of getting fit is, therefore, very personal, but it depends upon regular sessions at, say, a minimum of three times a week. The quality of each session must be tough enough to be effective, though not so demanding as to be completely exhausting. A useful judgement of when to increase the intensity is quite difficult at first, but experience in this area will build up over the weeks and months. Any increase in work effort is a good indication of fitness.

The performance of the chosen exercises should always be of the best quality, since there is not a great deal of value in a wild thrash of arms and legs. Each movement has a correct method and therefore a specific purpose.

The real incentive to progress is the inner sensation of health and vitality: the knowledge that it is doing good. Any chosen sport for which you are training will show signs of improvement. Stamina will enable a more prolonged effort. The gorgeous sensation of being healthy is addictive.

The measurement of fitness is not easy to record. To show how much of a problem this is, try to tell someone how fit you are. The scientists involved in sport have devised charts upon which are entered body functions and diet. Accurate graphic results can be shown in this way.

Resting heartrate is the easiest test to measure. As a general rule, if the heart beats slowly when resting (70 to 75 beats per minute) this is a healthy sign of general fitness. Of course the true method is to record regularly the heart beat when at complete rest, possibly shortly after waking up each morning. Keep a record over a period of weeks to see if there is a slight slowing down.

Another method is to find out how long it takes for the heart rate to return to normal after a vigorous session. A quickly falling rate indicates an improvement in basic cardiovascular fitness.

In order to keep at a constant level of fitness, provided this is not a high plateau, a quite light programme will do the trick. The tough part of the whole affair is the initial stage. Once a pattern is established, it is merely a matter of continuing with the sequence. Indeed, it is possible to reduce the amount of training considerably and still keep a good degree of basic fitness. This is accomplished by a topping-up process; a regular work-out twice a week will be sufficient to keep the body at just above normal condition, although most people become rather more involved than this and want to reach a higher level.

As with most things which are good for you, and give pleasure and a sense of accomplishment, there is an addictive result. Fitness can be taken to infinity. There is not a measurable limit. What can it be like to have super-fitness? Few of us will ever know. It is possible to become so involved, at any age, that you are never satisfied with the result. Perhaps this is not the best idea. A healthy attitude to the whole spectrum of training for sport is to assess what level you are seeking. When working out reaches a point at which you are content, but still hungry for a little more, then the right level has been achieved.

General fitness remains in the system for a very long time. It is easy to maintain a low level of healthy condition without much stress or effort once the body has enjoyed a good fitness programme, and a person who has reached a good level of fitness will retain some of that health and vitality for months or even years. Sports fitness has an accumulative effect, although it cannot be stored up for the next year or more. What does occur, is that the basic functions of the body have been used properly and continue to work efficiently long after training has slowed down or ceased.

General muscle strength lasts longest, and flexibility of joints is also retained for a long time. Good circulation is usually maintained for a very extended time. The first noticeable reduction in fitness after a prolonged lay-off is respiration. Breathing is so easy to notice that we are aware of any changes immediately. A daily aerobic session of about ten minutes will soon improve the breathing to a good level.

Fitness eventually becomes a natural part of life. The planning of sessions and watching improvements in yourself is a fascinating hobby. Anyone can control their physique, fitness, weight and health. The vibrant beauty of health cannot be measured, only envied and admired.

2 Exercises

GENERAL AND SPECIFIC FITNESS EXERCISES

It is important to choose activities which are appropriate to your needs, and there is a great deal of fun and value to be gained from just trying out some of the movements, shapes and skills. The best method is to analyse what results you are seeking and then put together a few exercises to make up a session.

Perhaps the warm-ups in Chapter 1 would be quite enough for a beginner; the fitter person ought to be capable of a good warm-up followed by a strong session and warm-down. Progress from beginner to more expert is covered later in the book.

1 **Step-ups** (*Fig. 4*)

Use the stairs, or a kitchen chair, perhaps a low stool of about 15-18in (38-45cm) high.

When stepping up the stairs, speed is the byword. When stepping on and off a chair or stool, because of the increased height, a slower effort is required.

This is a simple, continuous, stepping up and down exercise. You may alternate the leading (first leg to step up) leg throughout the effort. The body should be held upright, rather than bucking forward as the first knee is picked up. The arms can be used for balance. A general warm-up and fitness exercise, it can be very aerobic if done quickly. The thigh muscles will soon begin to ache and then a tendency may be to cheat by pushing with the hands on the legs. Try not to give in to the temptation. Twenty step-ups is a good beginning, but this may be too much for a novice.

4 Step-ups

5 Running the stairs

2 **Running the stairs** (*Fig. 5*)

Run two stairs at a time on the way up. Run, rather than stretch-walk, to the top. The return journey must be under control. Make the effort neat and sharp rather than a mindless thrash of arms and legs. Obviously the amount of work will depend greatly upon the type of staircase in your home. The heart, lungs and muscles will be puffing and working hard. After three journeys up and down you may be tempted to use the bannisters to help in pulling up-hill. It is better to rest for a few moments and then repeat the sequence with top-quality style.

3 **Burpees** (*Fig. 6*)

This exercise was specifically designed by the armed forces to create a large work effort in a small space, and it is ideal as a general fitness exercise.

Begin by standing with the feet together. Next, drop down to a crouch with the hands on the floor, shoot the legs back into a front support position, then immediately jump the knees forwards to resume the crouch shape. Now jump high. Repeat the sequence. All the movements should be vigorous and continuous. The heart, lungs and most muscles will be working hard. After about fifteen repetitions, it is easy to cheat by shortening all the actions. As with all good exercising, the best results come from good quality rather than huge quantity. It is therefore best to break exercises down into manageable amounts. An increase will come as fitness improves.

6 Burpees

7 Squat thrusts

4 **Squat thrusts** (*Fig. 7*)

This exercise involves the crouch. With hands on the floor, and front support posture, simply shoot (jump) the legs backwards and forwards. Beware the fault of making short stubby actions. The support position is quite demanding on the shoulder muscles. During the exercise the tummy muscles and lower back (buttocks) are quite strongly stressed, making it very useful as a fitness and strengthening exercise. Twenty-five good squat thrusts ought to be a beginner's aim.

8 Stretch jumps

5 **Stretch jumps** (*Fig. 8*)

Begin by crouching, taking care to bend at the knees and hips. Touch the floor with the finger tips, and immediately spring up to a full stretch to touch the ceiling. Land and sink into the crouch; jump again at once. As with burpees, this is a continuous and demanding series of vigorous actions. The leg muscles are particularly under stress. (The store of blood around the gut area is dispersed for use elsewhere.) A good start would be 30 stretch jumps until the fitness level rises to allow an increase in jumps.

6 **Body circling** (*Fig. 9*)

This is a very loose, complete, all-action, smooth exercise. In order to obtain the correct shapes throughout the movement, there should be no stiffness in the legs and hips. As the body rotates with the arms raised, so the hips should circle loosely. The circling action can be in a vertical plane (like the hands of a clock) or in a near horizontal way, similar to a helicopter rotor. The effect should be an all-moving, circling, action without stiffness at any time.

This is a good general stretching warm-up, warm-down exercise. The repetitions for this exercise can very enormously, because the actions are so ideal for loosening up and stretching, but five circles to the right and five to the left is quite enough.

9 Body circling

10 Running on the spot

7 **Running on the spot** (*Fig. 10*)

This can be an easy option – but don't allow it to be. The running action should be alternately vigorous (not stamping) and light. Knee lift can be varied in height and speed. Keep the body upright and avoid the temptation to buckle forwards during quick running. The period of time for this exercise should be steadily increased with each session. Beware not to take it easy when extending the time period.

The heart and lungs will work hard in this exercise, and it is an excellent aerobic way of conditioning yourself. Fast-tempo music may well help you keep the pace, as well as adding to the enjoyment.

If you tend to shake the ornaments from the mantlepiece when running on the spot, try to lighten the action and aim for quality rather than clumsy vigour. The time allowed for running on the spot obviously depends upon how hard you make the effort. One minute is a good start, increasing to three minutes at the same level of effort after four weeks of training.

8 **Sit-ups** (*Fig. 11*)

All torso-curling sit-up exercises use the rectus abdominus muscles. It is absolutely vital, therefore, that in this type of movement the torso is curled by tucking the chin in and rolling the chest up. The same shapes should be maintained when unrolling. The speed can be experimented with; indeed fast movements need use only the top third of the action. Slower sit-ups ought to cover the complete range of the exercise. If you use a flat back shape in the course of sit-ups, too much stress is placed on the lower spine. The very nature of all sit-up exercises involves the surface abdominal muscles. Without stomach strength there can be only minor progress in practically all fitness work. The tummy muscles are the core element in human strength and fitness. They act in so many ways when running, jumping, swimming, etc., that the priority to all fitness workers should be to perfect sit-ups.

A beginner ought to be able to manage 20 good, steady, curling sit-ups. When a really fit person does this exercise it should be quick and non-stop up to 50 repetitions.

11 Sit-ups with variations

Sit-up with twist or straight

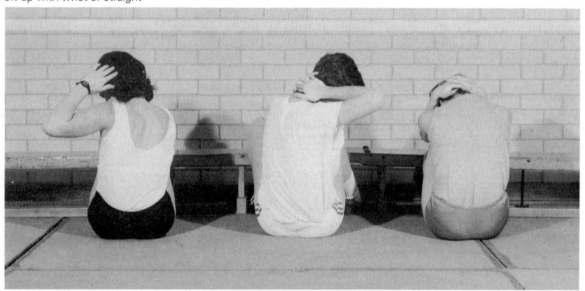

Elbow to knee sit-up

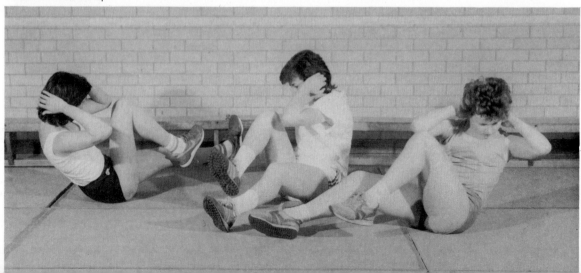

Roll-around sit-up

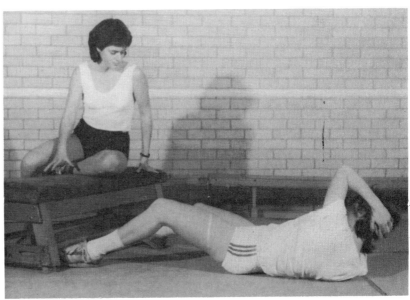

Feet-high sit-up (*and over*)

Knee grabs

Held abdominal balance

9 **Side bends** (*Fig. 12*)

A stretching exercise, this will benefit the whole of the rib cage and shoulders. Both arms, with hands linked, are pressed high above the head. The side bend action is initiated by pressing the hips sideways so that all the weight is on the outside foot. Then, and only then, can the body bend over to the side with the arms fully stretched above the head. The weight remains on the outside foot. The stretch effect is along the whole of the outside curve of the body.

This movement is excellent for warming-up, and also for relaxing after a good training session. Up to six side bend stretches to the left and right will help to ease the muscles and joints in the shoulders and torso.

12 Side bends

10 **Hip circling** (*Fig. 13*)

Stand upright with the feet placed no wider than the hips. Rest the hands on the hips. Rotate the middle torso in maximum circles without too much movement of the head.

This action is for lower back and hip flexibility and is a useful restful exercise to be used when recovering from the more vigorous exercises.

13 Hip circling

11 **Yoga twists (seated)** (*Fig. 14*)

This purely restful flexibility exercise is for the spine. One leg crosses the other with the bent-leg foot on the floor beside the straight-leg knee. If the left leg crosses the right, then twist to the left; the opposite is true for the right leg cross. When twisting, look backwards to use the whole spinal column. Keep the back straight and squeeze round gently in the twisting movement. Three or four twists to each side should be enough to release any tension in the back.

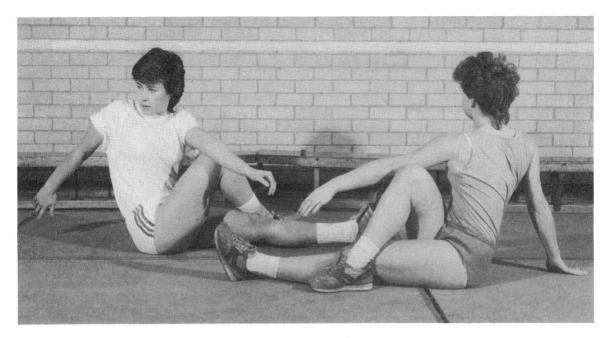

14 Yoga twists

15 Hurdle shapes

12 **Hurdle shapes** (*Fig. 15*)

The athlete uses these shapes to exercise the hip joints and hamstrings. Many variations are possible. The particular effect is to rotate the hip joint of the bent leg and stretch the hamstrings of the straight leg. Fig. 15 shows the basic shapes and what movements can be achieved. This type of exercise can be used between more vigorous activities to relax and stretch the muscles and joints of the hips.

Press over the bent leg

Press over the long leg

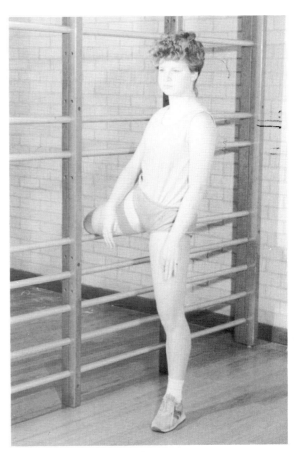

Standing hurdle stretch

13 **Leg lifting and circling** (*Fig. 16*)

This includes leg circles with the knees bent or straight, and leg lifts with curl, or straight side-to-side knee lifts. The particular muscles involved in these exercises are deep abdominal in location and are called the psoas. All leg-raising and circling movements also cause the surface muscles of the tummy to tense very firmly. Whether lying down (on the back) or standing (running, jumping etc.), when the legs move the psoas muscles are in powerful contraction. To strengthen this region the illustrations (Fig. 16) give explicit information.

The deeper muscles of the abdomen are often neglected because they cannot be seen or felt. The psoas group performs hidden duties, and without strength in this region it is not easy to run fast or even to have good posture.

In general, a fit and strong midriff is the basis to a well-balanced physique.

16 Leg lifting and circling

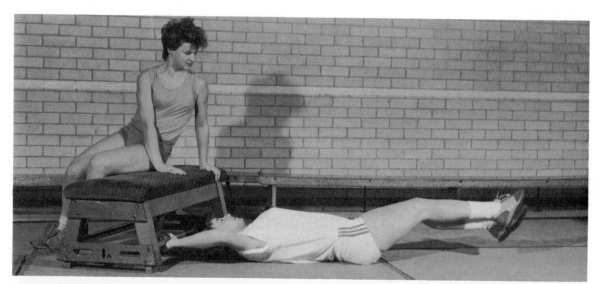

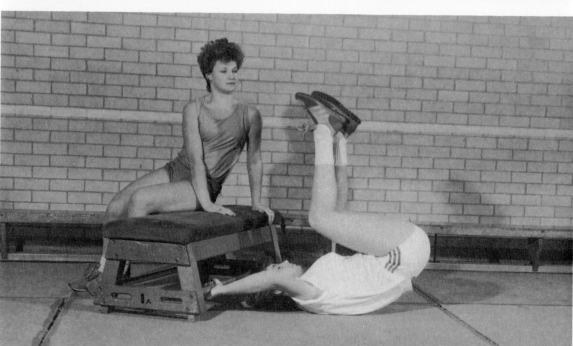

Side to side
bent legs

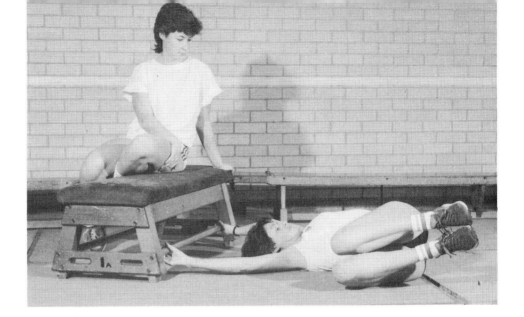

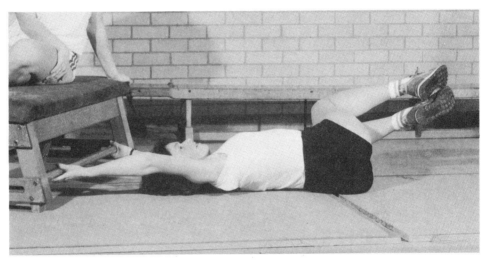

Straight leg circles (*and over*)

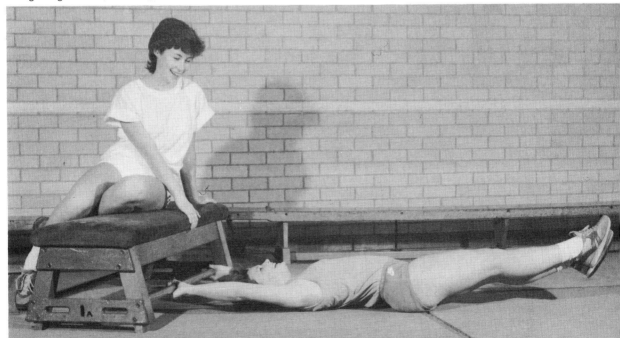

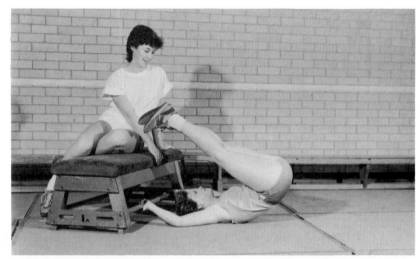

Straight leg lifts

Bent leg lifts

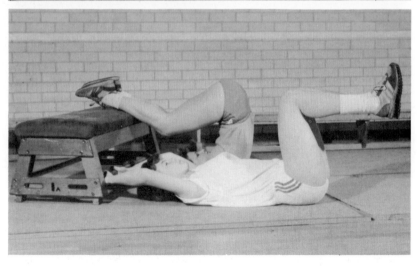

14 **Dips (legs assisting/angled)** (*Fig. 17*)

Arm, chest and shoulder muscles are not regarded as a woman's great strength, and the dips shown reduce the amount of weight actually lifted. Use a full range of movement and allow the armpits to sink as low as the hands in the deep position. Press out, trying not to cheat by over-helping with the legs. A certain discipline is necessary here. The width of the hand-hold can be varied: wide hand grip affects the chest (pectoral) muscles, whilst a narrower grip uses the arm muscles more.

It is difficult to recommend how many repetitions to do, since, when the arms and shoulders become tired, there is a tendency to give more and more help from the legs. Six dips could be your maximum before the legs start to give extra boost.

Angled dips

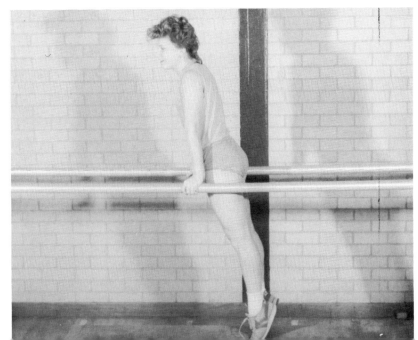

Bent leg dips

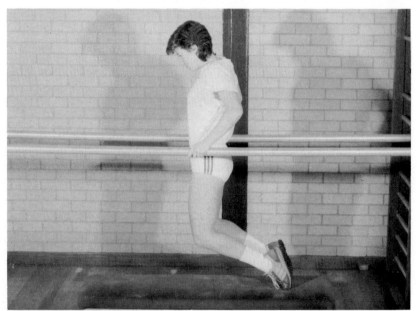

15 **Deep-dip press-ups/cat lick press-ups** (*Fig. 18*)

Arm strength, or lack of it, makes some traditional exercises impossible. Variations on the theme of press-ups enables weaker arm muscles to be fully used, and thus strengthened.

In deep-dip press-ups (Fig. 18) the beginning body support shape is easy to hold. From this beginning, bend the arms to the point where you feel you can support your body weight with difficulty; hold this position for a few seconds. Recover for a few moments in a front support and then try again.

Cat lick press-ups have the same start shape. Press the shoulders (with the arms straight) back and down (towards the feet). With a slight bend of the arms, attempt to slide forwards as though a cat licking the cream from a saucer, and end in a support position. Repeat frequently for arm and shoulder strength. The maintenance of the support position has a further useful effect – that of good stomach muscle tensioning.

Here again the difficulty is to prescribe an exact number of presses. We are so variable in shoulder strength, and, while some women can barely manage one press, others will find it easy. If it is easy for you, then 12 presses would be a good number to work from; on the other hand, three efforts may be the limit. After a few weeks of practice, the number will automatically rise.

18 Press-ups and variations

Cat-lick press-ups

16 **Hamstring stretch** (*Fig. 19*)

The hamstring muscles at the back of the thighs are frequently a cause for concern – cramp and muscle pulls happen in this region quite often – and regular stretching of these muscles will prevent problems. Hamstring stretching (or touching your toes) can be done seated or standing, and is best performed by curling the spine. The hands can grasp the ankles to pull down when you become more expert.

A stretching action of this sort should not be performed in a jerky, pumping way, since this will tear fibres and cause injury. All stretching should be progressive and calm, and the tissues exercised carefully and firmly. At all costs avoid the temptation to tug yourself into shapes. It takes months of quality exercising to improve flexibility.

An exercise such as the hamstring stretch can be used at frequent intervals during training sessions to relax and remove tension from leg muscles.

19 Hamstring stretch

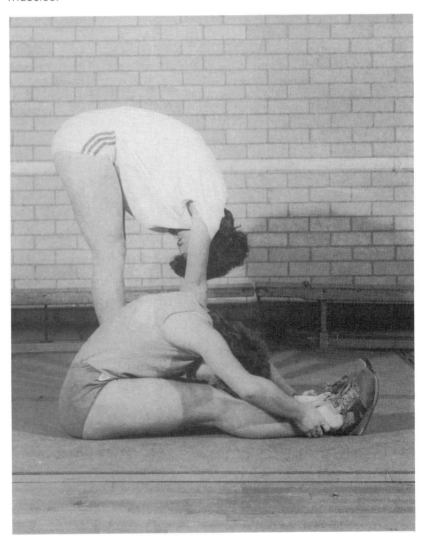

17 Arching (*Fig. 20*)

The spine has a vast variety of movements: arching, twisting, curling, and any combination of these. The spine is a truly versatile joint, and the muscles which are used in these exercises are numerous. When the whole length of the back bone, from the neck to the lower pelvis, is fully exercised, many aggravating back pains will disappear.

Back pains seem to form the largest category of sports injuries. In view of this, arching must be practised very carefully. At no time should a beginner try the advanced shapes straight away. A gentle start progressing over a period of months to more expert levels will ensure that no back pains arise from exercising.

Arching in all forms needs a simple recovery exercise to relieve any tensions. After any arch shape you should curl up into a ball, to relax the tendons and muscles. In this way your body can be stretched into a very extended shape and relaxed by a completely opposite form, that is to say fully stretched in the arch and completely flexed in the tuck.

20 Arching

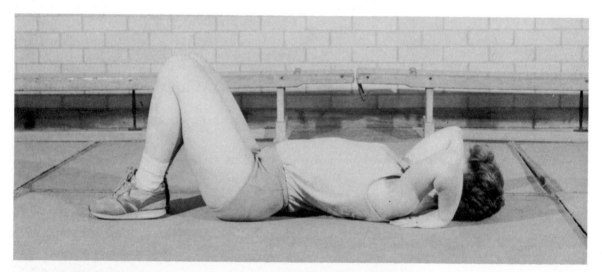

Shoulder arch

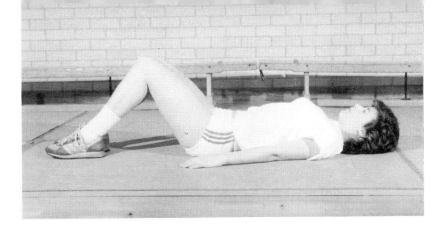

With knee lift

Front-lying twist arch

Ankle grasp arch

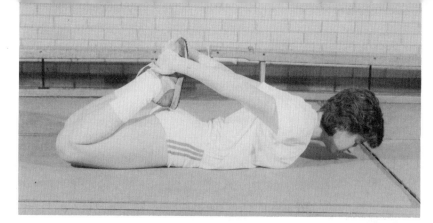

Partner assisted arch

18 **Leg swings** (*Fig. 21*)

This is very much a ballet type set of movements. The trunk remains upright throughout all the sequences. Leg swings can have many varieties. The general effect is for top thigh strengthening and flexibility of the hips. A happy side effect is to trim the buttocks and upper thighs.

The illustration shows several varieties of leg swinging. It is noticeable how the demonstrator keeps the standing leg almost straight and this makes the hips and thighs work more efficiently.

This is an excellent way of relaxing between other more routine exercises.

21 Leg swings

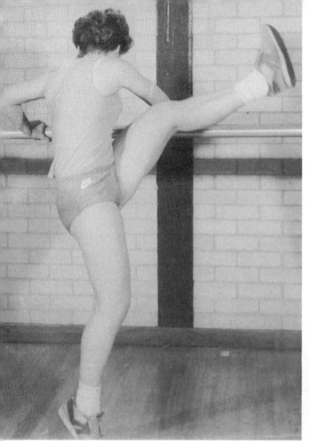

19 **Knee wagging** (*Fig. 22*)

Sit on the floor with your back straight. Draw the feet to the crutch with the soles of the feet together. Wag the knees up and down. This flexibility exercise for the hip joints can be used as a recovery between very active efforts.

Most women are quite flexible in this movement. It was said earlier that stretching should not be pumped and jerked. This exercise tends to break that rule, and so care must be taken to wag the knees smoothly to avoid pulling the hip joints too harshly.

22 Knee wagging

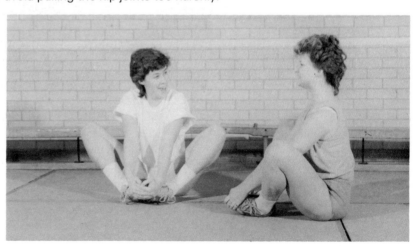

20 Side-to-side squats (*Fig. 23*)

Position the feet at double shoulder width. Squat down on one leg and curl the body forwards deeply between the knees. Change to squat on the other leg without rising too much between each squat. As with all squatting movements there is a secondary effect of encouraging the unused blood store in the abdomen to move out to the muscles of the body. Side-to-side squats help flex the lower back and stretch the hip joints

This particular exercise is a good method of stretching part way through a warm-up routine.

23 Side to side squats

21 **Shoulder balances** (*Fig. 24*)

In all shoulder balances the hips must be pressed vertically above the shoulders. Cycling, circling and general leg movements must be balanced in shape and attempt to reach the maximum amount of travel possible. There may be a certain difficulty in shoulder balancing initially. In the early days it may well be helpful to lean against some support furniture or apparatus to help you hold the balance.

24 Shoulder balances

Lunge

Splits

Side-splits

22 **Side leg raises** (*Fig. 25*)

Lie on one side supporting the head in the hand, elbow bent. Stretch the legs out very long. Raise the top leg vertically to maximum height without bending. This should be repeated frequently; then adjust the position to work the other leg. A thigh strengthening, slimming and tensioning exercise: as many as 30 leg raises to each side is a good number to aim for.

25 Side leg raises

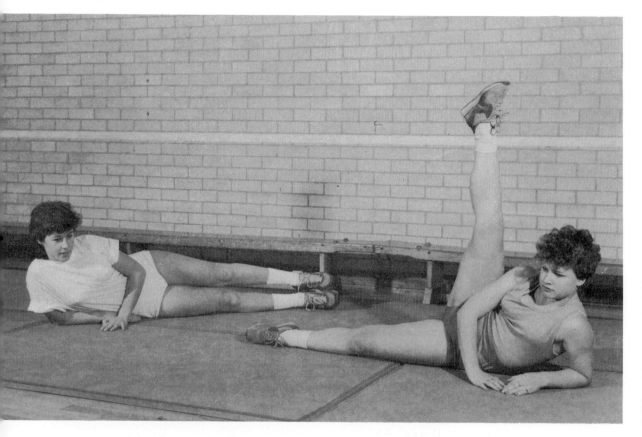

23 **Shoulder flexing and stretching** (*Fig. 26*)

The shoulder girdle is capable of an enormous variety and complexity of movements. The range of exercises is, therefore, equally full of variety; maximum range is the keynote.

The shrugging and curling of the shoulder girdle is very beneficial to the muscles and joints of the upper body. One particular arm fling exercise – the double arm swing jumps – requires high energy and concentration.

All arm and shoulder exercises are very useful for posture, breathing, and relaxation between aerobic efforts.

26 Shoulder flexing and stretching

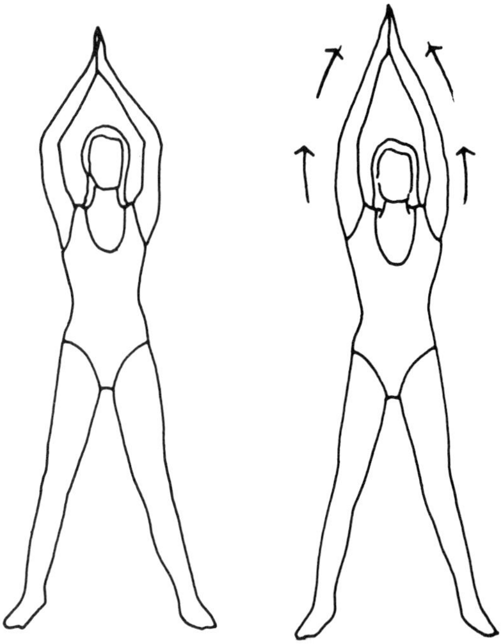

Shoulder press

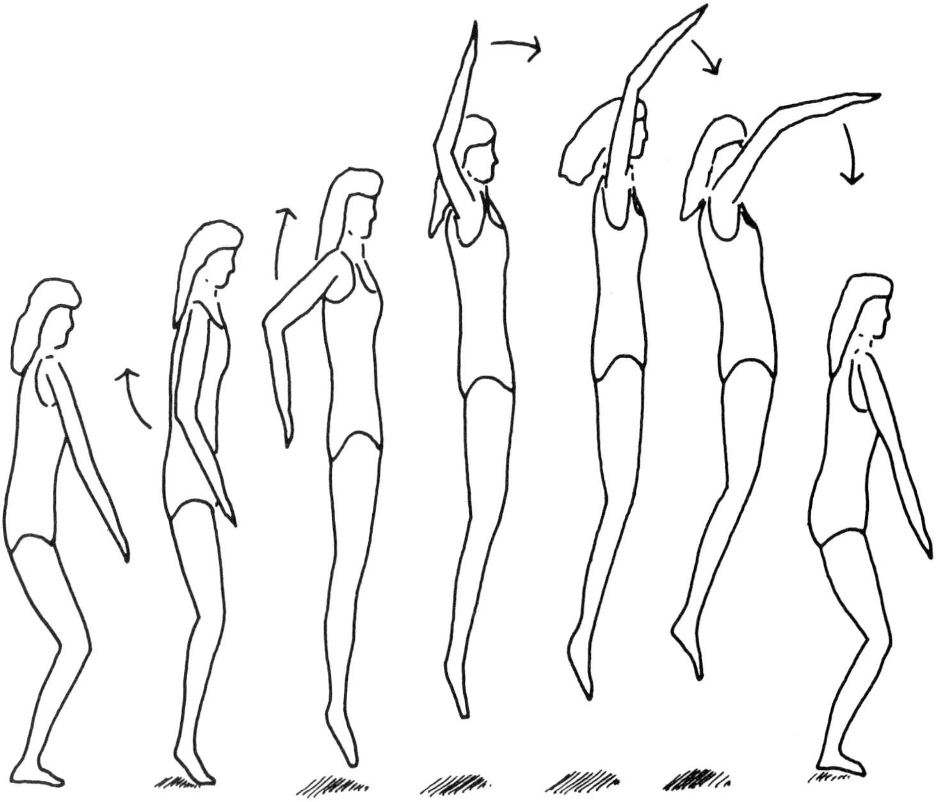

Double arm swing jumps

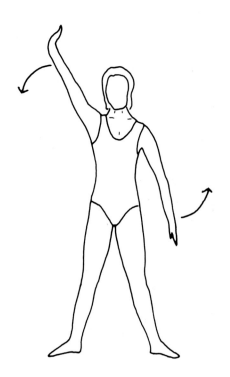

Shoulder flexing

Neck rolling and stretching

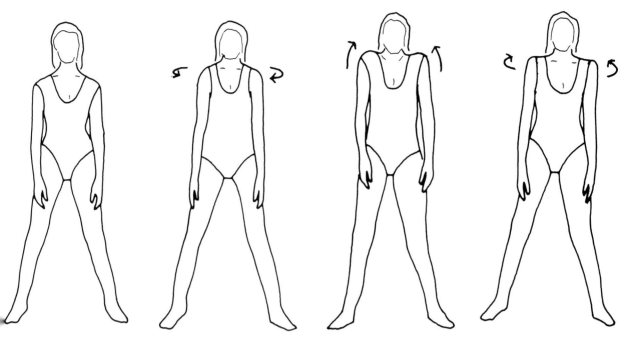

Shoulder shrugging and stretching

24 **Pectoral press and shoulder pull**

In both of these exercises the tension of the muscles must be held for about eight seconds. The position of the arms can be varied for different effects. The pectoral muscles respond rapidly to this press exercise (see *Muscle tensioning*, p. 12).

The complicated muscle structures in the shoulder girdle ought to be exercised regularly. The bustline and posture of the upper body will benefit from using these tensing actions.

In the pectoral press, the hands are held quite high and in front of the face. Keeping the elbows at shoulder level, press the palms of the hands together firmly.

The shoulder pull reverses the muscle action to work on the shoulders. In both cases the hands are kept as high as the chin.

The eight second press and pull demands a high level of concentration, especially in the last few moments before relaxation.

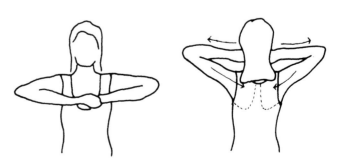

Pull, push muscle tension

25 **Lunges** (*Fig. 27*)

The aim is to stretch the hip joints, and thus the feet remain in the natural straight forward direction. If the back foot is turned to the side in the lunge shape, there is an undue strain on the ligaments of the rear knee.

Simply move into the lunge shape by taking a controlled long step forward. Bend the front knee and straighten the back one. The best effect is obtained by keeping the trunk upright and concentrating upon straightening the rear leg.

This is a good flexibility exercise and can be used to recover from some of the muscle building efforts.

27 Lunges

26 **Roll back jumps** (*Fig. 28*)

From the crouch, gently roll back on to the shoulders with the legs over the face. Roll forwards, bring the hands down beside the hips for balance and to aid the next move. Tuck the feet under the bottom and then jump vigorously up. As soon as you have landed continue into the squat recovery, leading into another back roll.

This is a gymnastic exercise which has good general muscle fitness effects, particularly for the legs. As few as five roll back jumps is quite enough for a beginner. It is a really vigorous exercise which takes a great deal of practice.

28 Roll back jumps

27 **Skipping** (*Fig. 29*)

Skipping is a varied and enjoyable method of improving your general condition. It is a pity that it has lost its popularity with the children of today. Skipping and running are very basic forms of fitness training.

29 Rope skipping

28 **Arm swing torso twists** (*Fig. 30*)

During the course of twisting the torso by flinging the arms at shoulder height from side to side, the hips must be held to the front. The waist is vigorously worked throughout the twisting movements.

30 Arm swing torso twists

29 **Standing lunge and hamstring stretch** (*Fig. 31*)

The bar should be close to waist height. Stand back from the support so that the split between the legs when the foot is on the bar is quite wide. Hold the bar with both hands and then progressively straighten the raised leg without releasing the bar. The effect is to loosen the hamstring muscles and stretch the lower back.

31 Standing lunge and hamstring stretch

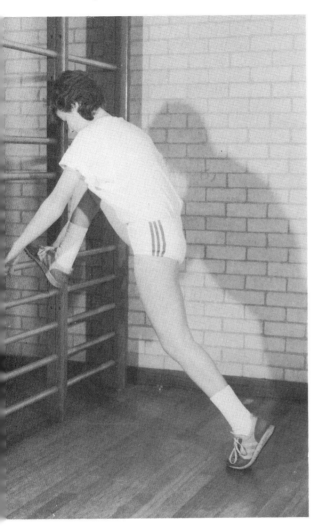

30 **Front lying torso twists** (*Fig. 32*)

This is a good flexibility exercise for the lower and middle back. The front lying position allows alternate twists to try to touch the outstretched hands with the foot.

32 Front lying torso twists

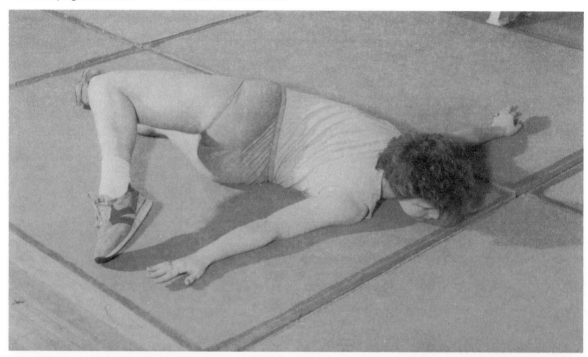

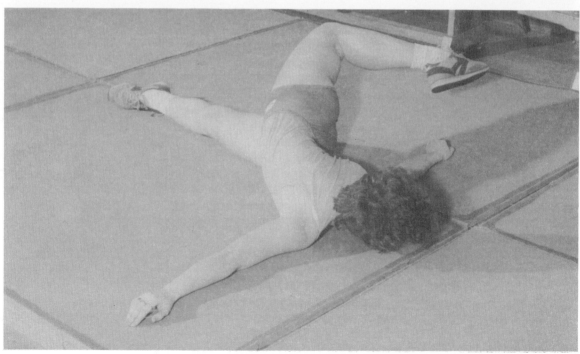

PARTNER EXERCISES

In order to make training more fun, exercises with a partner give a chance to chat and challenge.

Warm-up, stretching and strength work can be done using a helpful partner. The grip and supporting holds on each other do not require any special strength. After several practice goes you can mutually modify the exercises to suit your needs. After the first few tentative tries you will gain confidence and be able to work to each other's level.

In some of the exercises there is one worker, while the other passively holds or supports. Other routines allow both people to work hard at the same time.

Whether these ideas are tried at home or in the gymnasium it is a good method of comparing your abilities with someone else. It is often the case that, when static apparatus is in use, a partner could easily be your support rather than furniture or gym equipment.

Only a few exercises are shown here; you may well invent your own, or make improvements and variations on a theme.

Holds, grips and supports on each other ought not be too tight, but should give you confidence to work thoroughly. If stretches are being used where one partner pulls the other into a shape, take care not to be too heavy-handed. This is called passive stretching and should be under careful guidance: no one will thank you for inflicting an injury upon them.

1 **Leg circles** (*Fig. 33*)

These are for the tummy and deep abdominal muscles; an additional side effect is the strengthening of the chest muscles. The worker lies on her back with the arms stretched out on the floor. The supporter sits or lies in between the arms with her legs over one of the worker's hands and the body over the other hand. The worker can then circle the legs either straight or bent for five or six revolutions in each direction. You can then change places and continue with the exercise.

33 Leg circles

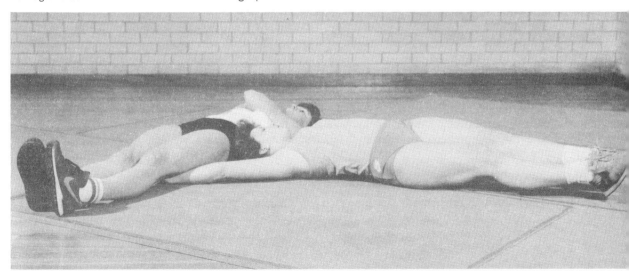

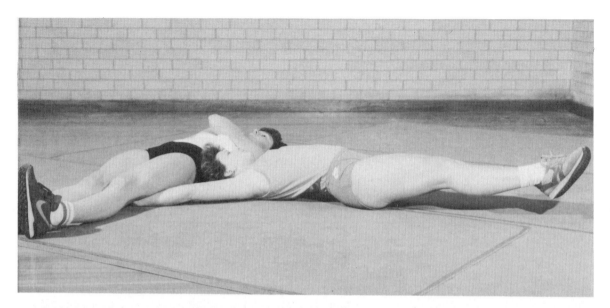

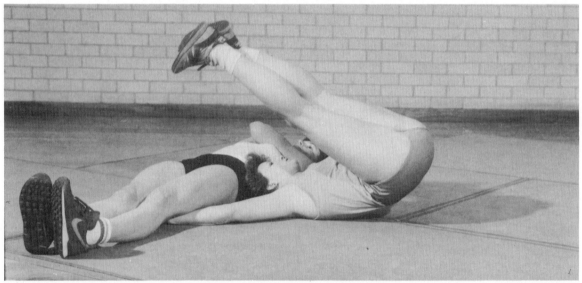

2/3 **Split rocking and hurdle rocking** (*Fig. 34*)

These are a variation on the same theme. In both cases the effect is to stretch the hamstrings and loosen the lower back.

Sit facing each other with the legs split sideways. Put your feet against those of your partner (the legs ought to make a square). Reach forward and hold hands. Gently rock, one person to lie back, the other to bend forwards. Keep the legs as straight as possible throughout the movements. If the hurdle sitting shape is preferred, you must alternate the long leg so that the bent leg of one of the partners and the foot of the straight leg of the other participant meet foot to knee. A dozen rocking backwards and forwards movements is the recommended dose.

34a Hurdle rocking

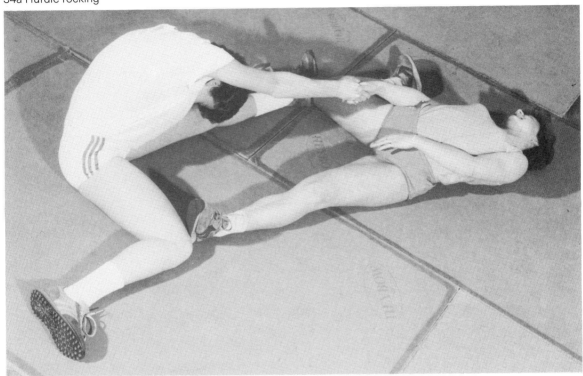

34b Split rocking

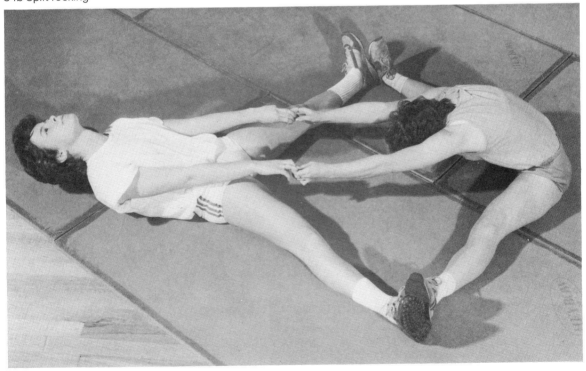

4 Hand link leg lifts (Fig. 35)

These will strengthen the tummy, thighs and chest muscles. Lie flat on your back with heads towards each other. Reach up and grasp each other's hands. Simultaneously lift your legs up to touch your feet with your partner's. This can be done with legs bent or straight. After some practice, the timing of the movements can be judged by a slight pull on each other's hands. Fifteen repetitions of the movement will work your tummy.

35 Hand link leg lifts

5 **Leg-interlocked sit-ups** (*Fig. 36*)

Sit on the floor facing your partner for this tummy exercise. Interlock the legs by overlapping legs and feet. One person sits up at a time. By alternating the sit-ups the legs remain trapped. In order to create a greater amount of work, the hands can add weight by being behind your neck. Twenty sit-ups for each person.

36 Leg-interlocked sit-ups

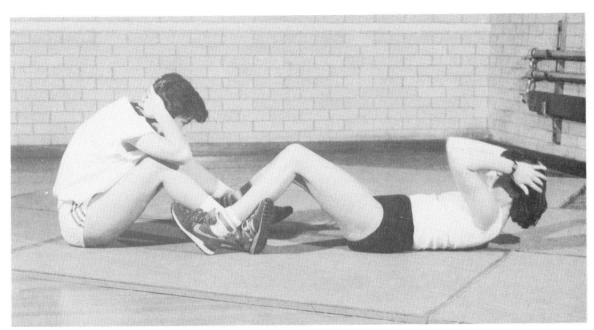

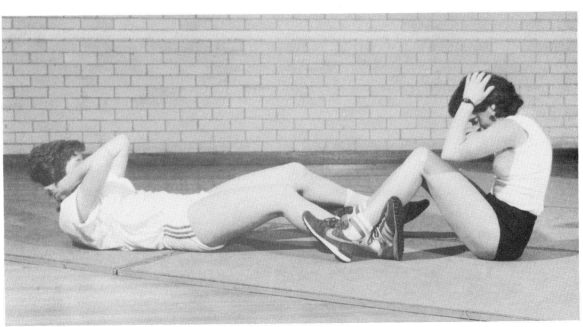

6 **Round the circle sit-ups** (*Fig. 37*)

These are for the oblique tummy muscles. The worker sits with legs comfortably astride. The supporter holds the ankles with hands or by resting in a lounging position over the worker's shins. The exerciser then rolls the torso around in large circles by moving to the side and rolling off the elbow to sit forwards. The bigger the circle, the better the effect. Try six circles to each side, then change places with your supporter.

37 Round the circle sit-ups

7 **Leg lift shoots** (*Fig. 38*)

This is a general purpose tummy and front of the body exercise. The worker lies on her back. The supporter stands near the worker's head, and holds a careful standing balance. The worker reaches back and grasps the supporter's ankles. You are now ready to begin. Roll the knees to the chest and shoot the legs up straight into a shoulder balance. Return to the starting shape and repeat 15 times. Change places, and, whilst one works, the other recovers.

38 Leg lift shoots

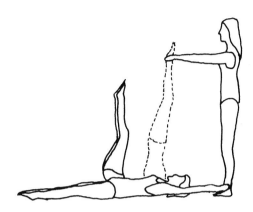

8 **Sit-up/stand-up** (*Fig. 39*)

This is a general tummy and upper-leg toner and strengthener. Much of the responsibility for success depends upon the supporter, who must assist with the vital stand-up movement. The helper sits with legs astride. The worker stands in the 'V' gap of the legs with feet just under the seated person's thighs. The supporter holds the worker behind the calves. The action should now be continuous. The victim squats down and, in a very controlled manner, gently rolls back onto the floor. The moment you have unrolled, reverse the whole shape. Tuck forwards in a normal sit-up towards your partner. Now is the key moment for the supporter to make the exercise possible. A gentle pull on the calves of the worker will allow them to stand-up. Immediately the sequence has been completed it should be repeated, at least eight times.

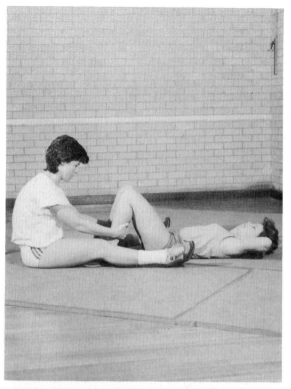
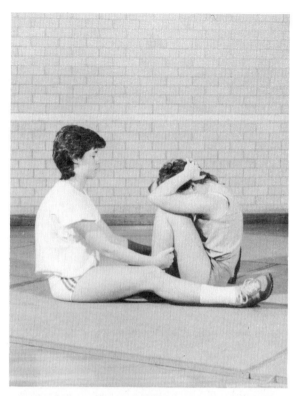

39 Sit-up/stand-up

40 Back-to-back standing
twists

9 **Back-to-back standing twists** (*Fig. 40*)

These are good for general torso flexibility and shoulder stretch. Stand back-to-back with a 12in (30cm) gap between you. Hold each other's hands high above your heads. The feet and hips should hardly move at all. Turn the top half of the body to the same side so that both chests face one side. Swing the arms back over the top and twist to the other side. Try ten twists to each side. The same twist movements can be done when sitting back-to-back with the legs astride.

67

10 **Leg lifts front lying** (*Fig. 41*)

A simple hand-to-hand grasp to support your partner will allow alternate people to raise either one leg at a time or both. The muscles of the buttocks and lower back will be strongly used. This can be repeated up to 20 times, and, as with all back exercises, it is advisable to recover by tucking into a ball to release the tension in the muscles of the spine.

41 Leg lifts front lying

3 Fitness schedules and circuits

FITNESS SCHEDULES

Fitness sessions at home can be very effective, and the floor space and furniture can be adapted in many ways as aids to exercise. Although your own home may not inspire you as much as a gymnasium, or keep-fit class, nearly all the rooms have potential for imaginative adaptation (Fig. 42 will give you some ideas). The key to successful sessions at home is planning a programme to suit your individual situation. Stages of planning can be best explained with a check-off list.

42 Household furniture as a gymnasium

Kitchen chair dips

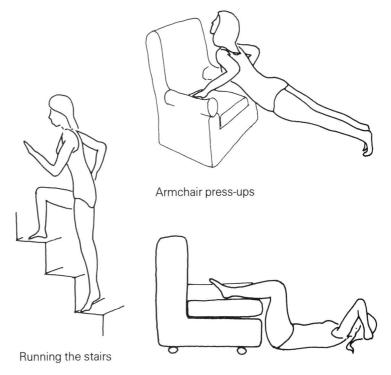

Running the stairs

Armchair press-ups

Armchair legs high sit-ups

Standing hurdle stretch

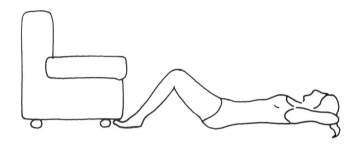

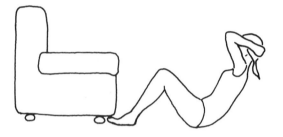

Armchair bent leg sit-ups or circling sit-ups

Kitchen chair step-ups

Supported shoulder balance

Running on the spot

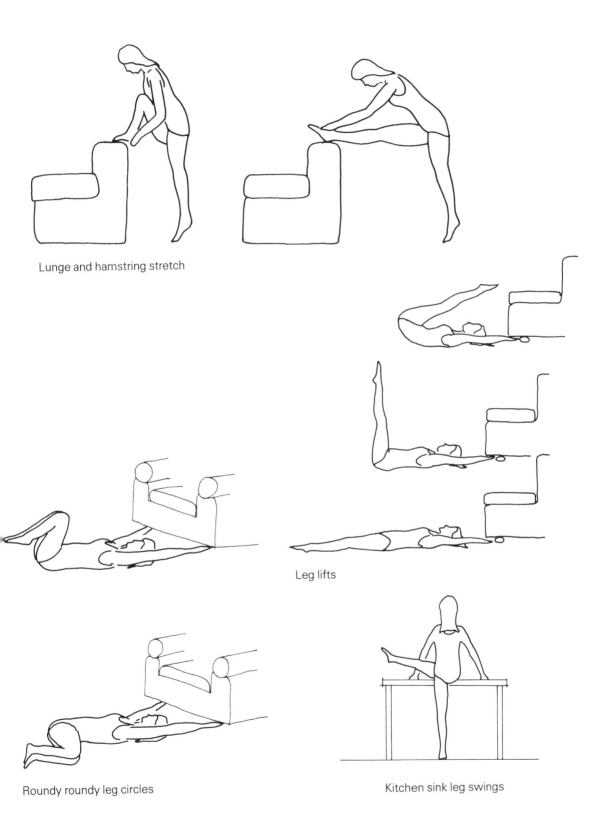

Lunge and hamstring stretch

Leg lifts

Roundy roundy leg circles

Kitchen sink leg swings

1 Decide which exercises are for you, and how long the session will last. Will you start with a jog or an indoor musical skipping warm-up?

2 Arrange your home gymnasium, clear a space, and decide what furniture will be in use. Is it safe?

3 Get dressed for action – a very purposeful act. You are now committed to take part.

4 Do it . . . warm-up; work out; work your body; warm-down.

5 Restore your home to its original state.

6 Shower and change.

Of these six steps to home fitness, only number four really matters. Once the planning stage is satisfactory, it is simple to set aside a period of time each day for your session. (Beware: it is addictive and you could easily get hooked.)

Session 1

Beginning to get fit is perhaps the greatest hurdle to overcome. Once you have decided to commit yourself to get really fit it is recommended to start without delay. Don't put it off until the weekend or wait for your friends to come to the same conclusion.

Even if you are already a sports player, but do not take any other form of fitness training, you must start gently. This is an initial fitness programme at beginner's level, and has a duration of three weeks (21 sessions).

The daily session starts with a fast walk or jog for a distance of 1½ miles. It will take, at the slowest, 15 minutes and should not cause too much distress for the first four runs, after which a bit more effort can be used. Be advised from this point that going too hard too soon is the worst possible start. Don't be panicked into running hard until your body is ready. The heart and lungs should work hard but without distress.

As soon as you get home, start the next part of the routine. There will be a strong temptation to sit down and rest; resist it, and go directly into general loosening and stretching exercises for a period of 10 minutes: trunk circling; arm and shoulder shrugging and circling; hip stretch lunges and tummy strength sit-ups.

The first run (or walk) was a gentle warm-up. It is now important to gently warm-down. It is suggested that a two minute jog on the spot (to music if you wish) would be a reasonable cool down, perhaps finishing with hip circling, or the gentle trunk circling which began the indoor session. Recovery is a steady lessening of effort and intensity, and not a complete stop.

A session of this type takes only 30 minutes – a very small price to pay. You will soon find the best time each day to do your training, although you should avoid working-out immediately after a meal.

There may well be some slight discomfort in the muscles the day after you start, but this will disappear with continual work. If you are badly out of condition it may be necessary to miss the second day in order to allow the muscles to recover from the first effort. (This should be the only session missed for this reason.)

It is possible to make a record of the session in the following way.

Activity	Notes

1 Jog (walk): 12 mins or 1½ miles

2 Trunk circling: 3 mins – 24, i.e. 6 to left, 6 to right, etc.

3 Arms and shoulders: 3 mins – 24, i.e. 6 to left, 6 to right, etc.

4 Lunges: 2 mins – 10, i.e. 5 with left leg fwd, 5 with right leg.

5 Sit-ups: 2 mins – 20, i.e. 10 sit-ups, 1 min rest; repeat

6 Warm-down: 5 mins – jogging on the spot

On days when the weather is appalling do not put off the run. A modification in the home is recommended. You could do 60 step-ups onto a low stool (about 15in [38cm] high), or even use the bottom two steps of the stairs. Perhaps as many as 90 or 120 step-ups could be tried by breaking the total down into groups of 30. Another substitute for running is rope skipping (perhaps to pop music), so much enjoyed by boxers.

After the fourth session a slight increase of effort will be needed. It could be that the easiest increasing method is to do a greater number of repetitions of the exercises, or speed up the movements.

There will be no visible change in physique for some time. On the other hand, you will begin to feel fitter and healthier. It is a good idea to measure critical areas of the physique before the first session. Record the information (secretly!). Regularly check these details, i.e. weight, waist and resting pulse rate.

At this stage a simple training chart can be drawn up on which you can plot increases and changes.

Exercise	Week 1	Week 2	Week 3 (etc.)
Run (jog)	10-12 mins	12-14 mins	15 mins
Trunk circles	24 (12+12)	30 (15+15)	30 (15+15)
Arms/shoulders	24 (12+12)	30 (15+15)	40 (20+20)
Lunges/leg swings	10 (5+5)	12 (6+6)	16 (8+8)
Sit-ups	20 (10+10)	30 (15+15)	36 (18+18)
Warm-down	5 mins		10 mins

At any time you can introduce a new exercise to build the session up from beginner level to more expert.

You would do well to refer frequently to the section of this book on exercises. Examine the problems you are trying to solve and select the exercises which suit your needs. This is especially important when choosing which movements are going to be the most beneficial to you. Once the sequence has been decided upon, do not change from exercise to exercise each day. Remain consistent for at least six sessions before any change is introduced.

After the first week a new exercise, or more, can be included (the warm-up and warm-down are always included as an automatic part of any work-out), for example:

1 Jog: 15 mins
2 Side-bends: 12 (6+6)
3 Sit-ups: 20
4 Skipping
5 Back lifts: 12
6 Trunk circles: 18 (9+9)
7 Jog on the spot: 3 mins
8 Hip circling/hamstring stretch

(Total time about 40 minutes)

This introductory session is suitable for all ages, and can be adapted to suit each individual. The pattern of regular sessions has a basic principle upon which to build the individual programme to suit you. If the running or exercises are too demanding, then reduce their intensity. Perhaps the number of repetitions in some activities is rather high: it is simple to lower that figure until you can handle more. As age increases, the speed with which progressively harder sessions can be introduced becomes slower.

The aim is to get fit for sport, and you may well decide that your sport is getting fit . . . and fitter, and fitter . . . this is a highly commendable attitude.

After three weeks of working at the initial fitness programme there will be a need to progress. Indeed, many people will by now have increased the quality and effort as the weeks speed by.

The progression to a higher level is best achieved by a change of session rather than by intensifying your present schedule. Exercising at times when not following the schedule is to be fully encouraged. A moment of spare time can always be usefully employed with a quick practice.

If you wish to train each day of the week you ought to consider alternating a hard session with a gentler programme. One important aspect of hard training is recovery. Sufficient time should be allowed for the body to restore and recoup its energy. Rest and work should be proportionately balanced.

The home has limitations when considering a really vigorous training programme. Running becomes a very important ingredient if you should wish to reach a good level.

Session 2

This is for those who are already taking part in a sport. It should be followed at least twice a week unless it conflicts with your sport; after all, 50 to 60 minutes is not a high demand. It may be a useful pre-season training programme, in which case four weekly sessions is the recommended dose.

At this level your individual needs must be assessed. A few careful thoughts about whether you are seeking speed, weight control, stamina, strength, etc. should help you to modify this session to suit you. The basic layout for a session of the type would be as follows:

1 10 mins stretch and exercise interspersed with rope skipping or jogging; warm-up
2 8-9 mins run (hard) 1½ miles (10 mins on a bad weather day)
3 6 mins vigorous tummy exercises
4 10 mins selected exercises for muscle strength and tension, according to your sports needs
5 6 mins selected flexibility exercises
6 4 mins jog ½ mile.
7 5 mins general flexibility exercises; warm-down

Your wisdom will now be tested to select the exercises which are most suitable. It is so easy to do only those movements which are fairly, or simply pleasantly, gentle. Getting fit, maintaining fitness and improving general condition is a very progressive sequence, and therefore this session should be followed for about 8-10 weeks.

These exercises for different areas of the body can all be performed in the home. Many movements have multiple effects and therefore may appear in different sections. You can 'pick and mix' a programme from the following lists.

1 *General*
   (a) Step-ups
   (b) Running the stairs at speed, two at a time etc.
   (c) Skipping (with a rope to music)
   (d) Running on the spot (variations) speed, high knees, etc.
   (e) Bob jumps on the spot
   (f) Jumping with double full arm swings
   (g) Burpees
   (h) Squat thrusts (super-star style)
   (i) Crouch stretch jumps, floor to ceiling touches
   (j) Body circling
   (k) Standing (i.e. not jumping) squat to full stretch
   (l) Roll back jumps

2 *Tummy*
   (a) Sit-ups (variations) twists, slopes etc.
   (b) Leg lifts (arms/hands holding furniture) single leg, curling etc.
   (c) Tummy muscle tensioning exercises (static)
   (d) Knee grabs (single, double)
   (e) Body circles (feet trapped lying down)

3 *Legs – buttocks – calves*
   (a)   Shoulder balance, cycle and leg shape variations
   (b)   Hurdle sitting, arching
   (c)   Leg swings (standing) variations
   (d)   Boat shapes (front lying)
   (e)   Back lifts
   (f)   Front lying leg lifts (double, single)
   (g)   Arching (variations)
   (h)   Muscle clenching and tensioning of thighs, hamstrings etc.
   (i)   Side to side squats
   (j)   Ankle circling
   (k)   Side lying leg lifts

4 *Torso*
   (a)   All the tummy exercises
   (b)   Side bends with full arm stretch
   (c)   Arm flinging and twisting of the trunk (hips fixed)
   (d)   Body circling (*General* j)
   (e)   Forward curl down to ankles (standing or seated)
   (f)   Hip circling
   (g)   Arching
   (h)   Back lifts
   (i)   Leg lifts
   (j)   Sitting yoga twists

5 *Shoulders*
   (a)   Arm circling (variations)
   (b)   Shoulder shrugging (variations, circling)
   (c)   Head and neck wagging, tipping, circling
   (d)   Across the chest hand press (pectoral muscles)
   (e)   Across the chest hand pull (shoulder muscles)
   (f)   Press ups – variations
   (g)   Dips – variations
   (h)   Pull-ups

Session 3
It is unlikely that the home is the best place for this session. Perhaps you can use your local sports centre or club house.

1   2 mile run – last 200 metres at a high effort (12-15 mins)
2   10 mins easy stretching, flexibility
3   5 mins tummy work
4   60 step-ups, kitchen chair height (non-stop)
5   5 mins stretching shoulders and hips
6   60 squat thrusts (30+30)
7   Easy jog for 1 mile
8   Gentle warm-down exercises

A session of this sort should take at least 1 hour. It is designed to create a high level of work and general endurance. A way of making the session more palatable is to arrange to train with friends or the members of your sports team. A little competition in training is highly recommended. The incentive to turn out and train is further promoted because others are expecting you to be on time and ready to work. The team support for each other's efforts, and encouragement when someone is feeling low, are good boosts to the session.

Whatever sport you are involved in, some analysis will be required in order to decide on the types of exercise that will be of greatest value. There is no escaping the fact that a very fit person will excel in sport, even if the fitness is not specific to a particular game or skill.

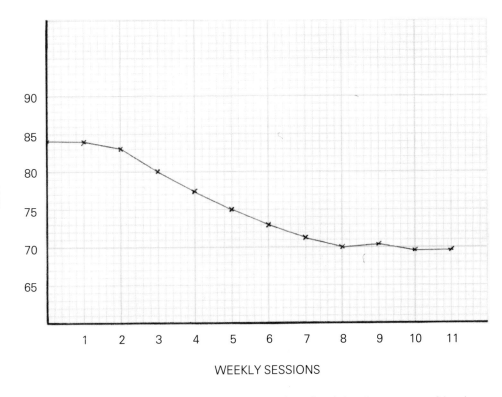

RESTING HEART RATE PER MINUTE

WEEKLY SESSIONS

43 Fitness graph

Fig. 43 is a result of eleven weeks of training for a team of hockey players in the off season. The ladies' ages were between 19 and 37 years. At the beginning of the programme all resting heart beats averaged out at 84 per minute, which may appear to be high. The readings were taken by the team members on each occasion. Even after careful checking there was no reason to disbelieve the figures. The resting heart beat in this case was taken in the pavilion immediately after each one had changed into sports gear.

Improvement in basic heart rate was very progressive for six weeks and then a plateau of little or no success set in. The team was involved in basic training for the first time. The graph shows an initial rapid improvement in basic heart rate. The ladies also managed considerable weight loss; in fact the team goal keeper achieved a staggering 1 stone 3lb (7.7kg) weight loss and had to buy a new track suit.

This pre-season programme involved running and exercising at a very basic beginner's level. The sessions were held once a week and lasted one hour, but many club members 'cheated' by training much more frequently.

The club has now set up a regular programme of fitness training on two evenings a week.

CIRCUITS (GYMNASIUM)

Circuit training is used by games teams and club players of any sport, and has been used by the armed forces for many years. The idea of this system is to use many exercises in a gymnasium for stamina, strength, speed, skill and flexibility. In fact the basic elements of fitness are blended together in a mixture of exercises. As with all fitness techniques, the key to success lies in how hard you work. Circuit training can be a very severe and strict task master.

The selection of exercises can be modified to suit the particular sport in which you are involved. The overall effect should be balanced, and thus the pattern of exercises must have variety, and the work sequence should move the emphasis of effort from one part of the body to another.

You should not do more than two consecutive exercises with the emphasis on one area of the physique.

There are many methods of structuring the circuit. The examples given range from introductory to Olympic level. Several different techniques are available of ensuring the right number of repetitions. The way recommended here allows 'workers' to go flat out and others to take part to their own level. Each exercise should be worked at for 25 seconds, regardless of fitness level. Allow about 5 seconds to change to the next discipline, and everyone taking part starts each exercise at the same time.

At first you may be capable of only one complete circuit. The aim is to reach a level of fitness when you can handle three continuous circuits. It is then time to modify the exercises to a slightly more difficult level, or to introduce new movements, and then progress to the next circuit.

Circuit 1 (for beginners) (*Fig. 44*)
Warm up
Jog 10 times around the gym, or do 5 minutes netball/basketball. General basic stretching exercises.

Exercises
Each is 25 seconds with 5 seconds for change-over recovery.

1 Step-ups
2 Sit-ups

44 Circuit 1

3 Jump pulls (bar height 15)
4 Gym length running
5 Back lifts
6 Bench jumps
7 Arm circles
8 Warm-down recovery (after 3rd circuit)

1 Step-ups

2 Sit-ups

3 Jump pulls

4 Sprints

5 Back lifts

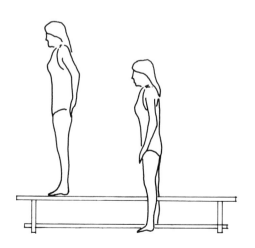

6 Astride bench jumps

7 Arm circling

Circuit 2 (intermediate level) (*Fig. 45*)
Warm-up sequence

Exercises
Each is 25 seconds with 5 seconds for change-over recovery.

1   Leg lifts
2   Burpees
3   Half pulls (bar height 9)
4   Knee grabs
5   Sprints
6   Jump pulls (bar height 15)
7   Back lifts
8   Sit-ups
9   Bench squat press
10 Warm-down recovery (after 3rd circuit)

45 Circuit 2

1 Leg lifts

2 Burpees

3 Half pulls

80

4 Knee grabs

5 Sprints

6 Jump pulls

7 Back lifts

8 Sit-ups

9 Bench squat press

Circuit 3 (the tough one) (*Fig. 46*)
Warm-up sequence

Exercises
Each is 25 seconds with 5 seconds for change-over recovery.

1 Leg lifts
2 Burpees
3 Half pulls
4 Bench jumps
5 Press-ups
6 Jump pulls
7 Knee grabs
8 Sprints
9 Step-ups
10 Back lifts
11 Bench squats
12 Sit-ups
13 Deep jumps (sets of 3)
14 Warm-down (after 3rd circuit)

46 Circuit 3

Press-ups

Deep jumps

A subtle change in the order of exercises can place greater emphasis on different parts of the physique.

Some considerable organisation through your sports club is needed to set-up really effective circuit training. A physical education teacher is a priority, and there are rules governing the use of gymnasiums and the apparatus. A P.E. teacher has all the necessary qualifications. The club secretary will have to book the gymnasium well in advance and arrange payment.

A willing time-keeper and whistle-blower is the only added extra to keep the sequence of exercises and change-over times under control.

Warm-up and warm-down is best achieved in the team group. The comradeship of a large squad working out is quite a spur to continuity and excellence. A little competition during training tends to make everyone reach for an extra special effort.

The circuits described here are suitable for a large number of sports enthusiasts to train at the same time. There should be enough room for three people to work at each discipline.

Circuit training is a method of gaining fitness for absolutely any sport. There are no exclusions for age or type of physique. The key to it all is your work rate. If you put in the effort, the results will come.

CIRCUIT TRAINING EXERCISES

Half pulls (bar height 9) (*Fig. 47*)
This is a shoulder girdle strengthening exercise. The hands hold the bar at a comfortable width, and the body stretches out under the bar. There should be only a slight bend in the body so that your bottom is just above the floor. The action is to pull up on the bar. At the top of the pull your chest should touch the bar; when you sink down, allow the arms to go completely straight, and then repeat the pull-up.

47 Half pulls

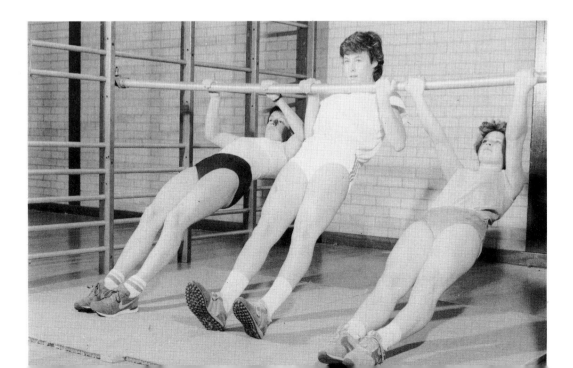

48 Bench jumps

Bench jumps (*Fig. 48*)
Stand astride a gym bench, and then make rapid on/off jumps, the feet landing on either side of the bench.

Jump pulls (bar height 15) (*Fig. 49*)
Grasp the bar which should be just above head height. Jump and pull continuously. Try to jump and pull high enough so that your chin is above the bar. This exercise should be vigorous and rapid.

49 Jump pulls

Bench squat-press (*Fig. 50*)

Use a gym bench hooked to the wall-bars at about 6ft (1.8m) high for this general strengthening exercise. Hold the end of the bench in the palms of the hands, as if ready to press it above your head. This is a very dynamic set of movements. Sink down into a squat, then stand up and press the bench high. Continue to repeat the actions.

50 Bench squat-press

Deep jumps (*Fig. 51*)

This exercise is a leg strengthener: a series of evenly spaced jumps which start from a crouch, spring into a fully-stretched flight and land to recover for the next jump. There should be little or no pause between each jump.

51 Deep jumps

Back lifts/leg lifts

These exercises all work the muscles of the back and buttocks. When the legs are lifted, the main emphasis is upon the very strong muscles of the buttocks, and the curl up of the back affects the muscles of the spine.

The movements ought to be as long as possible. Some people will find these activities very difficult due to lack of flexibility and good muscle tone. In general, the shapes should not be held for a prolonged time; a continuous repetition will give the best results.

52 Back lifts/leg lifts
Single leg lifts

Double leg lifts

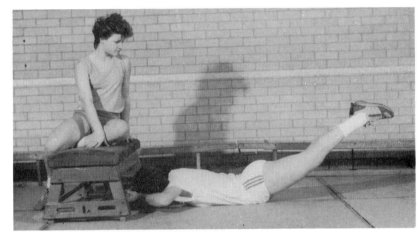

Back lifts

Boat shapes back lifts

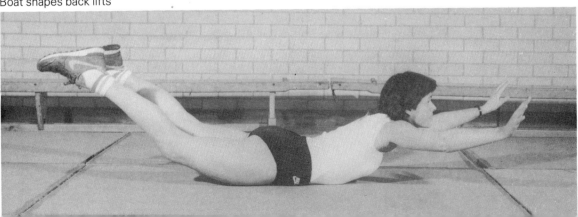

OUTDOORS

The attitude of going out in sports kit to run and exercise on the roads, streets and country pathways in Britain is fast becoming a national pastime, although we have not yet developed the more enlightened approach of Scandinavia and the USA where most towns provide a trim track or jogging route. These courses have regular pausing places with rustic or tubular outdoor apparatus for work-outs.

The great outdoors offers an incredibly varied set of fitness opportunities, of which running is the greatest. When out jogging or running hard, anyone can take a two minute pause to inject some variety into the session, with exercises and tummy work.

Any strong gate-post or fence is an ideal support for a multitude of exercises which perhaps need more room than the home permits.

A tree is a gymnasium. Sturdy branches can be used for swinging on and pull-ups for shoulder strengthening (and the shelter provided may well be a useful stopping place when out running in wet weather!).

Roads and paths are not really the best surfaces for running on, as a continuous, unrelenting running programme on concrete and tarmac can damage feet, ankles, shins, knees, hips and spine. Although a wise runner will take an obvious precaution of choosing footwear which is properly designed for this type of training, the best way to avoid these dangers is to use the roads sparingly. Soft surfaces such as grass, the beach and woodlands keep injuries to a low level and are generally free of traffic and fumes.

FREQUENCY AND DURATION OF SESSIONS

There are no hard and fast rules as to how long each fitness session should last, and quality rather than quantity is always the guiding rule. It is true to say that the principle of training which gives the best results uses regular and progressive sessions.

Many top sports women train hard each day, often enjoying two daily sessions, but your personal schedule will almost certainly be influenced by any job, family and household pressures that affect your life. If possible, your aim ought to be one session per day of about 45-60 minutes. A regular weekly pattern is the best way, although too many people consider that one work-out per week will do the trick. (There is an old adage about taking a 'daily dozen'.) A minimum sequence of training just to maintain general fitness would be two sessions per week, and so in order to increase the level of general condition either a greater number of work-outs or tougher sessions is essential.

Each training session should be hard enough to make you puff and sweat. As fitness improves, it will be easier to reach a high level of effort. It is not easy to judge how much work should be included in each session in the early days, and it is better to do slightly too little at first and then increase the load as time goes by. A record or diary of training ought to be kept. This is a useful reference when planning future sessions. As the pages fill up, it also becomes a spur to continue training.

Each week could be broken down in the following way:

Mon   Long run 2½ miles (18 mins); 10 mins flexibility exercises; 10 mins strength exercises; 5 mins warm-down. (45 mins)

Tues Team practice or match, i.e. badminton, netball, swimming, athletics, hockey etc. (1½ hrs)

Wed   Rest day

Thurs Circuit training: home or gymnasium. (45 mins)

Fri   Rest day

Sat   Match or practice

Sun   Match or practice

(This has a work load of 5½ hrs per week)

The rest day should be the day before a competition. Most teams have one match per week, usually at weekends, so the pattern of weekly training is set by competitions or matches. During the off season it is likely that only one rest day will be needed in a weekly programme: probably the day after the toughest session.

Team practices should be a good work-out with skills in the first part of the training and speed and stamina practices towards the end of the session. Your own training sessions should also challenge you. If you deliberately set out to have a soft work-out, be certain of your motives. Is it because of loss of interest or lack of inspiration, perhaps boredom? Fitness work is only effective if it is taken seriously and produces the right effects and results. Half-hearted training bears little fruit. The end products of gentle sessions are low grade results and disappointment, and sloppily-performed exercises may well result in injury.

Commitment to training on a regular pattern with a long-term plan becomes a life-style. If this is the case, then the frequency of training will be regular sessions for much of your life.

The media often give the impression that top games players and sports stars are endowed with super-human strength, talent and aggression, and whilst they are, of course, exceptionally blessed with all of these things, the aspect which needs emphasis is the amount of basic training which has gone on over the years, and the quantity of training which continues throughout their competitive careers.

4 Physiological gender differences

There have been endless comparisons between men and women in sport, and, whilst it is generally agreed that men have a greater sports capacity than women in those activities which favour strength, this assumption can not be made when measurements of stamina and skill are concerned.

The governing bodies of many sports have refused female participation for reasons that must have been very important at the time. The rules of athletics, for instance, excluded women from all stamina events until very recently. Now, however, it is evident that women can challenge men in many sports without special concessions. In the case of the improvement of running times, women have far out-stripped the male regime. In Britain it has taken women only 18 years to improve by nearly one hour in the marathon (i.e. 3hrs 27m 45secs in 1964, to 2hrs 29m 43secs in 1982), whilst men have taken the best part of 75 years to make the same improvement.

The natural core functions of the female of any species are different from the male, to the point of being almost opposite. Even in the lowest forms of life the female is especially adapted to create a continuation of her own kind. Her size is invariably smaller than the male, although there are some notable exceptions to this rule. In the warm-blooded creatures, maleness usually means large and strong: femaleness, small and soft.

When comparing the woman's sports ability with men there are obvious disadvantages for the lady. Perhaps the need for any comparison is pointless, and it is more appropriate to look at the immensely rapid advances made on all fronts in women's sports.

Athletics is a sport which allows close scrutiny. The statistics are well documented in all respects. Few women's records have remained unassailable for long, whereas the history of men's athletics achievement is scattered with many long-standing 'freak' performances. By way of an example, Jesse Owens' record for the long jump lasted for more than 25 years, and now Bob Beaman's performance has almost reached the same vintage. Yet the long jump event for women has been progressively improved over the last 40 years. No record has stood for more than 4 years, and seldom has the same competitor remained at the top of the world ranking list.

The skeletal frame of a woman is specially formed to allow her to reproduce. The need for bulky muscles and large bones is not the first priority, and the balance of strength between shoulders and hips (or arms and legs) is nowhere near equal. In man, however, the vastly greater muscular power of the shoulders is easy to see. Men have a need, in primitive society, to fight and hunt, for survival, and many sports have developed as a result of this primeval need. Women have taken up these sports without changing the format, and when comparisons are made, therefore, there is an inequality not only in strength but also in the suitability of the sport.

In the area of fitness training, therefore, the woman must adapt a few of the 'male' exercises to suit her basically different frame. In all but upper body strength work there is no need for any change in movements when exercising. There is obviously a need to change the amount of weight lifted or carried, because women do not have the same bulk of muscle as men. Women in sports fitness training need only slightly modified schedules and exercises to suit their physiques, since the response of the body is the same in both women and men, and only the degree of muscular development, which is due to hormonal controls, is different. In some cases drugs are introduced to achieve astounding results, though these 'cheat' all natural performances.

Another modification in training techniques has to be made when considering the age of the participant. Sport is available to all age groups and the desire to improve with practice and training does not appear to be only for the young.

Schedules and exercises must be planned to suit the age and ability of the people involved. Young bones and joints can be permanently damaged if too much severe training occurs before physical maturity.

SPORT AND MENSTRUATION

A woman's attitude to menstruation in the early years would appear to depend upon the information given to her by her mother and her friends. If the initial expectations are of pain, inconvenience and considerable distress, then these can be the result. In the event of a reasonably casual and matter-of-fact explanation, the expectations and results will apparently be less severe. Attitude, therefore, forms a real base to dealing with menstruation and sport.

More important than this is the actual pain or distress caused by periods. Every woman will have her own pain threshold, at which point she will decide whether to train or not. Period pains are real and can be debilitating. It is unfortunate that this is not always recognised by coaches and teachers.

It is true that active women appear to suffer the least from menstrual problems. Even so, the monthly pattern can be more than a nuisance, and may well affect the planning of your sports programme. A competition calendar will aid planning around menstruation. Obviously if the pain or flow is excessive, and if your work, sport or social life is suffering, there can be no alternative but to visit your doctor. Regardless of fears and attitudes to the Pill, this does give a certain control, and often a reduction in pain and flow.

Age is another controlling factor. The onset and settling down into a monthly pattern can be rather irregular when a young woman is just progressing in sport; and when the menopause is imminent, similar haphazard conditions prevail. Many woman give up sport because periods are so inconvenient.

The medical profession is usually sympathetic to try to ease or solve the difficulties, especially if you explain that your sports and general fitness is suffering to the point that you are unable to go on. Pain-killers specially aimed at period pains are very effective, and there is no need to suffer regularly, and in silence.

SPORT AND PREGNANCY

Child-bearing and menstruation are seldom taken into account in fitness training. In the first instance, a fit and healthy person will usually ride the storms and nuisances of pregnancy with far greater ease than the unfit. After the birth, the advice generally given is to rest and wait some weeks before returning to sports. Obviously the doctor's advice is correct, but the word 'rest' is open to interpretation.

Most women are concerned about the shape of their tummy muscles after childbirth. The abdomen has suffered some very dramatic changes in a comparitively short time, and the muscles are stretched and reluctant to return to their original state. The hospital physiotherapists do their best but it is up to you to use the exercises to get back into shape as soon as possible. The tummy muscles will shrink back to a certain extent, but they need help to return to their former tone. Unfortunately, in some cases the stretched skin never returns to its original elasticity.

Post-natal exercises and routines will probably be the last thing on a new mother's mind, since a new baby is very time-consuming, tiring and disruptive. A few minutes per day, however, is all that is needed to start to repair the tummy muscles. They have been stretched and seem to refuse to return to normal; in fact the whole body may appear to be irreparably damaged.

Simple exercises can be started at a very early stage. The best example of this is learning to tense the stomach muscles. If, when in bed, you gently try to raise the legs (or one leg at a time) against the resistance of the blankets, the tummy muscles will tense. Similarly, any attempt at lifting the trunk will again tense the tummy. As with all abdominal strengthening, the back should be curled in order to eliminate lower spine injury.

Initially there will be little or only slight improvement, but perseverance will reap rewards later. A gentle and progressive return to training over a period of months rather than weeks is the best method.

Some women return to everyday life and training extremely quickly after giving birth; for others it is a more lengthy process. Consultation with your doctor or visiting nurse should precede a return to full training. Please do not consider motherhood to be the end of your sport: many women go on to improve after becoming a mother.

5 Ailments, injuries and treatment

People who take part in sport are prone to occasional injuries. Particular sports tend to create their own special ailments, and popular names have been given to some of the more common pains.

Racket games create tennis elbow, in which the tendons around the elbow joint become inflamed and sore. When the stress of racket swinging becomes too much for the joint, fluids collect around the moving parts and the elbow feels as if it has seized up. Rest seems to cure the problem until the next time. An improvement in wrist strength and an increase of shoulder flexibility gives more long-term relief.

Footballers suffer with cartilage problems in the knees. The kicking action which violently straightens the leg quickly damages the knee joint.

In both of these cases the fierceness of the actions are beyond the normal stress expected.

The majority of sports injuries are accidental. Cricketers seem to suffer from numerous knocks from the hard ball, and hockey players' shins are a testament to the damage caused by stick and ball. The games of netball and basket ball are supposed to be non-contact, but collisions and falls cause numerous sprains and bruises.

Athletics has a wide variety of stresses and strains. The short events predominately cause muscle pulls. Sprinters, throwers and jumpers use extreme violence in their events and the stress can create severe muscle damage.

It is the immediate care and treatment of injuries which eventually allows the best recovery and early return to sport.

The joints in the skeleton are especially designed to last a lifetime, but mistreatment shortens their life-span. The worse type of abuse which causes many problems in later years is lack of exercise. The body is a natural machine which thrives on use, provided the exercises and sports are not taken to excess. A large number of injuries and ailments in sport are self-inficted — people become too keen and over-do the first few sessions, and the muscles and joints are unable to cope with the stress. A gradual build-up from simple beginnings to a good work-out should take months rather than a few weeks.

Muscles build in strength and endurance simply by working the body in a full range of movements. In all but a few cases mature adults have lost much of the easy flexibility present in childhood. After a period of regular, graduated, exercise the muscles will lengthen and strengthen and the joints will loosen. Then the body is capable of increasing the load, effort, and range of exercises.

When an injury occurs, nature has made all of us respond in a similar manner. The injury usually hurts – pain is designed to tell us to rest. Swelling often occurs at joints and in the tissues; this prevents the proper use of that limb and is nature's way of avoiding further damage.

The majority of injuries can either be avoided or treated immediately using commonsense. Serious injuries must, of course, be dealt with by medical staff or trained first-aiders. Severe bleeding, concussion, fractures, breaks and dislocations are beyond the expertise and ability of untrained personnel. Players injured in this way or suspected of serious damage are best taken to the nearest hospital, preferably by an ambulance.

Minor sprains and knocks can be dealt with on the spot by the application of cold water or ice. It can do little harm, and invariably helps considerably. Ice should not be pressed against the skin for a prolonged time or it will 'burn' the skin with almost the same effect as fire. The ice should be wrapped in a cloth and gently applied to the injury. Even with this protection the ice pack should not be left in place for longer than eight minutes. The cold reduces swelling and this automatically reduces discomfort. The player could well be recovered in ten minutes and safely return to the game. Ensure that she can move the joint through a full range by using muscles and not passively forcing the joint with hand pressure. It is always advisable to compare the amount of movement with the other limb.

Passive manipulation means pulling and pushing a joint through its range of movement. Unless you are fully trained this should be avoided. It may well cause further damage and, of course, unnecessary pain.

When an injurious collision occurs on the games field, you must decide who to treat first: the one who is writhing around or the person lying motionless. The player who is still is likely to need attention before the other one. Unconcious people should not be unceremoniously dragged off the pitch. Check their breathing passages are free and then call for expert help. If any delay is anticipated, keep the victim warm but do not scoop them up and cuddle them.

Heat should not be applied to wounds, as this will increase blood flow and swelling. A bad cut can be held together rather than packing it with lint or, worse still, using yards of sticking plaster.

Playing games, training, and exercise in general can cause nuisances rather than injury, especially muscle soreness. There can be few people who have not complained of stiffness after exercise. Most of the discomfort is caused by an increase in waste product (lactic acid) in the muscle. In order to reduce these wastes it is important to continue exercising and moving gently. The worst possible thing is to sit down and rest: your circulation will stagnate and the excessive wastes are not dispersed. A good brisk walk and jog with some loose exercises is the best remedy. The value of warming-down cannot be over-stressed.

Massage can help with some muscles, but should be used with care and only under expert guidance. It will sluice out the waste and reduce tension. The only person taking active exercise during massage is the masseuse, so don't be fooled into thinking that a massage is as good as an exercise session.

Mild embrocations are also helpful and modern ones do not smell like a stable. It is, however, still better to burn a little energy and exercise stiffness away. This will use up calories and open the lungs as well as prevent soreness in the muscles.

Strained ligaments and tendons occur if your stretching exercises take the joint beyond its limit of movement. Over a progressive period of calculated exercise all the skeletal joints will increase in range. Attempting advanced shapes and stretches before you are in the right state of preparation can be harmful. A joint should not be taken beyond that stage which you can actively achieve by your own muscle control. Passive stretching by a partner ought to be avoided unless you are under expert tuition. Repeated passive stretching may create long-term ligament strains which could take months to heal. Of course, a twisted ankle is an ideal example of strained ligaments, where a joint is forced beyond its normal limit. The pain, swelling and bruising is almost immediate, and can be treated initially by the application of cold water or an ice pack. Other ligament strains may be the result of long-term incorrect exercising and require equally long-term treatment.

Muscles can suddenly swell if worked too hard when lifting weights. It is usually quite painful and medical help is needed. The swelling and internal bleeding can be reduced by the ever-ready ice pack method. This is only first aid and an expert must be consulted as soon as possible after the muscle tear has been identified.

Bruising and compression of muscle and soft tissue often happens in sport. Usually the bruise does not show up until several hours after impact. Bruises are a light form of internal bleeding and can be relieved by using cold compresses at regular intervals throughout the following days. It is not unusual for a bruise to gravitate, or move down the limb, away from the initial injury. Often a sprained ankle will result in a blue-black faded line gradually working down to the sole of the foot and toes.

Wear and tear in the active joints of the skeleton can cause some very impressive cracking and grinding noises. There can also be sharp pain and aching sensations. The inflammation that accompanies these symptoms is known as osteo arthritis, and degenerative arthritis. They both mean a wearing and tearing within the joint. It may be alarming to be told that your joints are degenerating, but it happens as a natural process of ageing. The effect on each individual ranges from no pain or stiffness whatsoever to crippling disability. The majority of people barely notice any rapid or significant change over a long period.

Rapid joint degeneration can be reduced and delayed by following a regular routine of exercise. Overweight people tend to suffer with

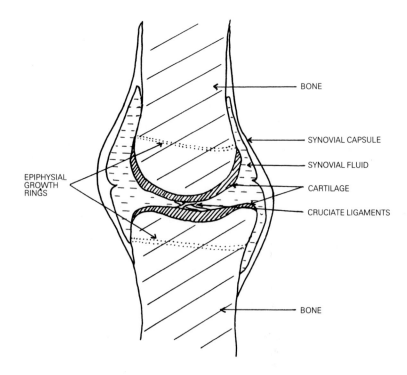

BONE

SYNOVIAL CAPSULE

SYNOVIAL FLUID

CARTILAGE

CRUCIATE LIGAMENTS

EPIPHYSIAL GROWTH RINGS

BONE

arthritic joints, as well as people who never stretch or exercise. Weak muscles also increase the likelihood of arthritic joints. This last point is a key part of a vicious circle: degenerating joints can be painful, and the discomfort does not encourage you to take exercise; thus the muscles atrophy still further and the joint takes more punishment. To break the circle, the muscles must be strengthened and the joints moved through a full range.

CONCLUSION

The medical profession is adamant about the value of regular exercise, provided the programme is well structured and sensibly balanced. They stress key points and it is worth looking at their sound advice.

Fitness programmes should start very easily and progress at a steady rate. Warming-up and warming-down must be a part of every session. Do not be afraid to drop-out if you are suffering pain or distressing breathlessness. If your instructor has no qualifications and shows no sympathy when you reach your limit, seek a different instructor.

The exercises in this book have already been tried and tested on various groups – ladies' hockey teams, men's rugby teams, international athletes – as well as a broad spectrum of women at keep-fit classes. We hope that you have enjoyed reading this book and that you have managed to put together a fitness programme that suits you or your team.